The NIATx Model

Process Improvement in Behavioral Health

David H.Gustafson, PhD

Kimberly A. Johnson, MS Ed, MBA

Victor Capoccia, PhD
Fran Cotter, MA, MPH
James H. Ford II, PhD
Don Holloway, PhD
Dean Lea
Dennis McCarty, PhD
Todd Molfenter, PhD
Betta Owens, MS

Center for Health Enhancement Systems Studies

University of Wisconsin–Madison

Madison, Wisconsin

David H. Gustafson, PhD, is Research Professor of Industrial and Systems Engineering at the University of Wisconsin–Madison and director of the Center for Health Enhancement Systems Studies, which includes NIATx. His interests in decision, change, and information theory come together in the design of systems and tools to help individuals and organizations make effective changes.

Kimberly A. Johnson, MS Ed, MBA, deputy director for NIATx, served for seven years as the director of the Office of Substance Abuse in Maine. She has also been an executive director of a treatment agency, managed intervention and prevention programs, and has worked as a child and family therapist.

Contributing Authors:

Victor Capoccia, PhD
Senior Scientist, NIATx

Fran Cotter, MA, MPH
Quality Improvement Team Leader, Division of Services Improvement
Center for Substance Abuse Treatment,
Substance Abuse and Mental Health Services Administration

James H. Ford II, PhD
Director of Research, NIATx

Don Holloway, PhD
NIATx Core Development Team

Dean Lea
NIATx Core Development Team

Dennis McCarty, PhD
Department of Public Health and Preventive Medicine
Oregon Health & Science University

Todd Molfenter, PhD
Co-Deputy Director, NIATx

Betta Owens, MS
NIATx Deputy Director, 2003–2007

Editor: Maureen Fitzgerald
Graphic Designer: Susann Ely
Cover Photography: Daniel Ely, Ely Design Group

NIATx
University of Wisconsin-Madison
4121 Mechanical Engineering
1513 University Avenue
Madison, WI 53706
www.niatx.net

ISBN: 978-0-615-58142-2

Awards from the National Institute on Drug Abuse (R01 DA018282) the Robert Wood Johnson Foundation (58190, 59714) and the Substance Abuse and Mental Health Services Administration (SC-05-109) supported the development and preparation of this manuscript.

Contributing Authors

Victor Capoccia, Senior Scientist, NIATx, holds a PhD in Health Policy from Brandeis University's Heller Graduate School. Previously, he directed the Open Society Institute's national initiative, Closing the Addiction Treatment Gap. Dr. Capoccia also led the Robert Wood Johnson Foundation's Addiction Prevention and Treatment team that initiated NIATx. For ten years, Dr. Capoccia directed CAB Health and Recovery Services, Inc., a community-based substance abuse treatment provider in Massachusetts.

Fran Cotter received a master's degree in political science from the University of Maryland and an MPH from Johns Hopkins University. Ms. Cotter is a Senior Public Health Advisor and Quality Improvement Team Lead with the Substance Abuse and Mental Health Services Administration. She oversees federal initiatives on quality measures and health reform and process improvement in behavioral health. She directed the SAMHSA Strengthening Treatment Access and Retention Program (STAR) project and collaborated with the Robert Wood Johnson Foundation in the creation of NIATx.

James H. Ford II, Director of Research at NIATx, earned his PhD in Health Systems Engineering from the University of Wisconsin–Madison. With more than 30 years of health care experience, he has used health systems engineering tools and techniques to study, support, and sustain organizational and operational change initiatives to improve health care service delivery. He also has extensive experience managing data systems across multiple health care organizations.

Don Holloway earned his PhD in Industrial Engineering from the University of Wisconsin–Madison. His diverse professional and academic roles focus on improving health care quality. Holloway helped develop the NIATx model and has served as a process improvement coach and consultant for multiple NIATx projects,

Dean Lea is an organizational and leadership development consultant, and a principal at the Burlington, Vermont-based Tupelo Group. Lea was a member of the original team that developed the NIATx model.

Dennis McCarty is a professor in the Department of Public Health and Preventive Medicine Oregon Health & Science University. He collaborates with policy makers in state and federal government and with community based programs to examine the organization, financing, and quality of publicly funded prevention and treatment services for alcohol and drug disorders.

Todd Molfenter, Co-Deputy Director of NIATx, earned his PhD in Industrial Engineering from the University of Wisconsin–Madison. Previously, he worked at the Institute for Healthcare Improvement, where he directed consulting services. Molfenter specializes in the use of organizational collaboratives as agents of change.

Betta Owens, consultant, earned a master's degree in business and marketing at the University of Wisconsin–Madison. She also holds a degree in social work. Owens served as NIATx Deputy Director from 2002-2007 and has served as a process improvement coach for multiple NIATx projects. An experienced trainer, she also leads NIATx Change Leader Academies and other training events, and mentors new NIATx coaches.

Acknowledgements

NIATx extends a special thanks to Molly Bennett for the writing services she provided in developing the manuscript for this book.

NIATx also gratefully acknowledges all the organizations and process improvement coaches that have shared data and success stories that support the effectiveness of the NIATx model. We appreciate all that we have learned from them.

CONTENTS

Introduction

Wer began NIATx in 2003 as a learning collaborative. Our goal was to help participating treatment centers develop and apply process improvement techniques to improve the quality of care they offered. When we began, we were working with 39 substance abuse treatment centers. By 2011, a network of over 2,500 agencies, from all across the country, in a variety of healthcare and public welfare industries, were using the NIATx model for process improvement to improve the services they offer their clients and establish efficient, productive business practices.

> NIATx is a pioneering process improvement center, part of the Center for Health Enhancement Systems Studies at the University of Wisconsin-Madison. Originally, NIATx was the acronym for The Network for the Improvement of Addiction Treatment. Today we are known simply as NIATx to represent our expansion into other areas of behavioral health as well as social services.

What we know from our experience is that the failure to get services has less to do with the client and his or her abilities and more to do with the way in which services are delivered. NIATx focuses on the service delivery system. If we know people are reluctant to use behavioral health services or that people involved with the criminal justice or child welfare systems come to those services involuntarily, then logically, the services need to be easy to access, easy to use, and engaging rather than forbidding. We founded NIATx on the conviction that what inhibits many organizations from delivering the kind of care they'd like to isn't resources or staff—it's problematic processes in the work system.

What do we mean when we refer to an agency's processes? Simply put, a process is the series of actions taken to produce a particular outcome. For example, when a potential client picks up the phone to call your agency seeking help, that's one step in a process whose outcome is the scheduled appointment. The way that an agency does business—its work system—is the sum of its processes. And when an outcome regularly is not achieved (i.e., the client doesn't get services), it indicates that there is a flaw somewhere in the process—not in the client, not in the staff person completing the process, but in the process itself.

Knowing this, we established NIATx with the belief that substance abuse treatment organizations, and subsequently the other types of organizations that have also adopted our practices, could improve their services by redesigning their work systems using process improvement techniques. By identifying the internal practices and processes that inhibit its ability to provide effective, timely care, an agency could then make changes to those processes to eliminate those problems and make progress toward improvement.

Of course, it's easy to acknowledge the need for improvement; it's far more difficult to determine exactly how to do it, especially in an environment where time and resources are scarce, and improvement often seems impossible. Knowing this, we developed a model for process improvement that could serve as a straightforward guide for service organizations seeking to improve their processes and provide better services for more people. In our model, an organization sets out a goal for improvement, and then examines its internal processes to determine how they might be changed to make that goal a reality. There are no complicated data elements to collect, no levels of training, nothing that requires staff to take a couple weeks off from their scheduled duties to flow chart and redesign the workflow. This model is simple, streamlined, and adaptable by organizations with few resources.

What the NIATx Model Does

Improvement is a vague concept. It's possible to recognize the need for improvement without knowing exactly what that improvement would look like. What makes some services better than others?

To reach a goal, you need to know how to define the problem and identify what an acceptable level of improvement is. Clearly defining a goal is the first step toward determining which actions will need to be taken to get there. A key component of the NIATx model is that it removes ambiguities surrounding the word "improvement" by clearly defining concrete, measurable objectives.

Since the beginning of NIATx, we've defined improvement, in our context, as increasing access to and retention in services. Access to services and retention in services are key problems of addiction treatment, mental illness treatment, and rehabilitation for people involved in criminal activities.

The NIATx Aims

Because we know that specific goals lead to manageable, doable projects, NIATx organizations initiate change projects that target one of four specific aims:

1. Reduce Waiting Time (the time elapsed between the first call for help and the first service)

2. Reduce No-shows (the percentage of scheduled appointments that are missed)

3. Increase Continuation (the percentage of clients who remain in treatment through the fourth treatment session)

4. Increase Admissions (the number of people admitted into the program)

   These four aims are considered the "original" NIATx aims. As the NIATx model has matured, addiction treatment organizations have used it to target other aims, such as improving "handoffs" between levels of care, increasing the use of evidence-based practices, or improving their billing systems. We'll discuss these in Chapter 3.

The way we see it, the goal of a service organization is to do everything it can to make the client's experience as smooth and easy as possible. This is particularly necessary when the need for the service is generated by illness or other problems that people would rather not address. A service organization must identify the barriers clients face—the reasons why they don't enter treatment or services, don't make it to appointments, or drop out early—and change the processes involved to eliminate these barriers and replace them with processes that facilitate, rather than inhibit, access and retention.

The NIATx Principles

The NIATx model, and indeed our philosophy toward change, is driven by five principles that have been shown to be the hallmarks of successful improvement projects. As you'll learn in Chapter 2, we developed these principles through an analysis of decades' worth of research, across a number of industries, of why certain projects fail while others succeed. These five principles are the underlying structure upon which NIATx change projects are built and when applied effectively, they will give a project the solid foundation it needs to succeed. You'll learn more about the five principles, and how we developed them, in Chapter 2. Here, we give you a quick introduction.

Principle 1: Understand and Involve the Customer

Understanding and involving the customer is the single most important action you can take to set up your project for success. In fact, our analysis showed that this one principle has a greater impact on success than the other four combined. Lose sight of your customer (your client) and you lose sight of success.

3

Principle 2: Fix Key Problems

If a change project is to be successful, it needs the full support of the agency's leadership, and the way to ensure that support is by addressing the problems that truly matter to the CEO.

Principle 3: Choose a Powerful Change leader

In a NIATx change project, a staff team works together to find solutions to the problems that are holding the organization back from its targeted aim. At the helm of this group is the change leader, who manages the team, runs the project's day-to-day operations, and serves as the liaison between the team and the organization's leadership. In this delicate position, the change leader must be many things to many people: she must have the CEO's ear, and be close enough to ask for and receive resources needed for the project; she must have the respect of her peers and subordinates; and she must possess leadership and motivational skills.

Principle 4: Get Ideas from Outside the Field

Developing innovative solutions to entrenched problems often requires looking beyond the boundaries of the familiar and shaking things up a bit. Looking at the practices of other industries is a way to push beyond these boundaries, and it's often there that you'll find the best ideas.

Principle 5: Use Rapid-Cycle Testing

NIATx change projects are structured around what we call "rapid-cycle" testing. Rapid-cycle testing consists of a series of change cycles conducted in quick succession. Change teams test potential changes to an existing process and evaluate the results using P(lan) D(o) S(tudy) A(ct) Cycles: Plan the change, Do the test, Study the results, and Act on your conclusions[1]. The key is that these tests are conducted quickly, on a small scale, over a short period of time. Throughout, the change team collects data related to the targeted aim to measure progress. The data also helps the team to refine and retest a promising change on an incrementally larger scale before adopting it completely.

> Rapid-Cycle Testing refers to a series of PDSA Cycles conducted in rapid succession. Change teams test potential changes to an existing process, evaluate the results, then adopt, adapt, or abandon the change.

NIATx is based on the premise of gradual improvement over time. Improvement isn't usually accomplished by one big change; it's a series of smaller changes, tested and implemented one at a time, that add up to a big impact.

The NIATx model works because:

- Short, small-scale tests are less disruptive to clients and staff, and are low-risk in the sense that little time and resources will be expended on trying out changes that quickly prove to be ineffective.

- Evaluating changes both quantitatively (through data measurement) and qualitatively (through team discussion of how the test went, and input from clients and staff) produces changes that both improve the targeted aim and can be feasibly implemented within the existing system.

- A new process can be perfected in repeated cycles before it is implemented on a full scale.

- The low-risk, no-commitment nature of quick tests encourages creative experimentation.

- Each cycle builds on the previous ones, as each cycle yields knowledge to apply in future tests.

Data collection may sound intimidating, but we purposefully encourage agencies to keep it simple. Done properly, data collection should be clarifying, not confusing. You'll find detailed instructions on how to establish measures and collect data in Chapter 7.

An Overview of the NIATx Model

Now that you've learned about some of the key concepts behind the NIATx model, we give a brief overview of the model itself so you can see those concepts in action.
Consider this an introduction—you'll learn about each component of the model in greater detail later in the book.

The Key Players

The executive sponsor: A member of the organization's top management (often the CEO) who makes a firm commitment to the change project, secures necessary resources, and helps guide the project.

The change leader: Chosen by the executive sponsor, the change leader directs the day-to-day operations of the change project, manages the team and keeps the executive sponsor informed of the team's progress.

The change team: A group of staff and clients or former clients from throughout the organization assembled by the executive sponsor to brainstorm potential changes and organize and carry out rapid-cycle tests—under the supervision of the change leader.

Steps in the NIATx Model

1. Define the Project: The executive sponsor (or the CEO, if not the same) chooses an aim to serve as the project objective. Sometimes it will be easy to identify which aim to focus on; in most cases, the executive sponsor may use the walk-through as a tool to understand where the agency's biggest problems lie.

2. Conduct a Walk-through: The walk-through is a valuable tool for gaining insight into your customers' needs and determining which of those needs are not being adequately met. During the walk-through, the executive sponsor (and possibly the change leader or another key project stakeholder) takes on the role of client and physically goes through every step that the typical client would, including the initial call for help, the assessment and/or intake process, and paperwork. The purpose of the walk-through is to get a new perspective on your organization's services by seeing them through the customer's eyes. Your observations may help you understand which aspects of your organization work for the customer, and which ones a change project could work to improve. The walk-through also solicits ideas and opinions from staff, adding yet another valuable perspective to the picture. You'll learn more about the walk-through in Chapter 4.

3. Define Improvement Measures and Collect Baseline Data: NIATx change projects are outcome-driven, which means that changes are evaluated in large part by whether they produce demonstrable, measurable improvement. Before starting a change project, then, the team must decide what criteria they will use to measure progress; i.e., which data will most accurately reflect performance levels with regard to the targeted aim. For example, for a project aimed at reducing no-shows to assessments, the measurement might be the percentage of clients who fail to show up for a scheduled appointment.

Before beginning testing, the change team must measure the organization's current levels of performance, so that they can compare testing data to determine whether the change is producing an improvement. We call this pre-testing data baseline data, and it can also be used to set a numerical goal for the project (say, reducing the no-show rate from a baseline of 45 percent to 15 percent). Chapter 9 discussed data in greater detail.

4. Rapid-Cycle Testing: The bulk of the project is devoted to brainstorming process changes that could potentially improve the project's aim, and then using rapid-cycle testing on these changes—one change at a time—to check their effectiveness. As mentioned above, these "rapid-cycle" tests are conducted on a small scale, over a short period of time, in rapid succession. The team uses Plan-Do-Study-Act (PDSA) Cycles to implement the promising change on a small scale (maybe on only a handful of clients) for a short time (often a few days). During the test, the team collects data using the same method it used for collecting baseline data. At the end of the testing period, the team discusses how it went, evaluates the data, and decides how to proceed. If the change seems promising but didn't produce great results, the team can tweak and retest the change. This cycle of refinement continues until the process change yields maximal improvement, and all the kinks have been worked out. Once the team has perfected the change, it can be adopted across the organization.

Alternatively, if a change being tested fails to yield improvement and doesn't seem promising or workable, the team may choose to abandon it and move on to the next rapid-cycle pilot test. Because pilot tests are so short and are done on a small scale, there is little risk involved and nothing is lost. A change team can learn a lot, however from a failed test.

> NIATx recommends that change teams use a form like Change Project Form (see Chapter 5) to record their progress. You can also download this form and others from the Forms and Templates page of the NIATx website at www.niatx.net.

5. Implement Changes and Sustain the Gain: Once a change has undergone rapid-cycle testing, all the kinks have been worked out, and it has been adapted to fit neatly into the work system, it's implemented on a full scale. Staff are trained in the new procedure, written procedures are updated, and everyone in the organization is alerted to the change.

But while adopting a change is cause for celebration, it's not the end of the challenge. In fact, sustaining a change—ensuring the new process is properly carried out and that it continues to produce the improved outcome—requires as much effort as creating it. It's easy to slip back into the old way of doing things if you're not paying attention, so during the sustainability phase, the organization continues to monitor the process and measure outcomes in an effort to standardize the new process and assimilate it into the work system. During this phase, the key is to make it as easy as possible to use the new process, and as difficult as possible to go back to the old way of doing things.

The NIATx Model

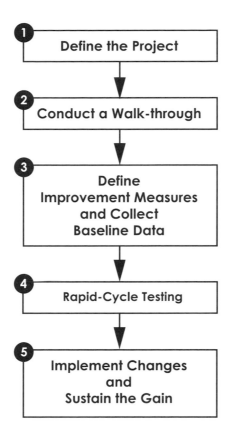

1. **Define the Project**

2. **Conduct a Walk-through**

3. **Define Improvement Measures and Collect Baseline Data**

4. **Rapid-Cycle Testing**

5. **Implement Changes and Sustain the Gain**

A Culture of Continuous Improvement

Organizations use the NIATx model to make progress toward specific goals, but process improvement doesn't end with a single change project. The larger purpose of change projects is to create an organization-wide culture of continuous improvement.

This means celebrating accomplishments without becoming complacent. It means always thinking of what could be done better and, once you've accomplished that, how you could improve the process even more.

In an organization with a culture of continuous improvement, everyone is constantly thinking of creative, innovative solutions for improvement. It's a place where people are equipped with the knowledge and resources to conduct their own mini pilot tests or collect their own data. And it's a place where there is a company-wide commitment to making improvements stick.

A successful change project does more than increase admissions or reduce no-shows—it shows the organization's leadership and staff that change is possible, that improvement is within reach, and that successful process change benefits everyone. In short, a successful change project engenders enthusiasm for more change and more improvement.

This is important because improvement is difficult in the face of disinterest from above (the CEO or other top leadership) and resistance from below (direct service employees). A successful project engages staff, soliciting their input and creating avenues to get everyone involved. Providing this opportunity for involvement serves to counteract the notion some staff may have that change is something to be feared, that it will have a negative impact on their work lives, that they have no say in what's going to happen, or that their viewpoints aren't being considered. Most people experience change in the workplace as bad because it is top-down, and often seems sudden and unexpected. Engaging staff and clients in the process of improving services makes change more dynamic and inclusive and reduces the elements of change that people have come to fear in the workplace.

Successful improvement projects change not only processes, they also change attitudes. They extinguish the idea that improvement is impossible, that change is daunting, and that frustrations and inefficiencies are an inescapable part of the business and nothing can be done about them. In the new way of thinking, everyone, from the CEO to the front desk staff, views obstacles as opportunities for improvement, and they're willing to put in the work because they have confidence in the outcome.

The NIATx Community

Peer networking is an important part of our philosophy, and NIATx organizations experience the many benefits that accompany being a part of the community we have built. By connecting with the organizations using our model, we create opportunities for personalized support and guidance. Instead of giving an organization a NIATx manual and leaving it to carry out a change project on its own, we actively engage them by offering coaching, answering questions, and helping them overcome obstacles, and plan for the next steps.

Interactivity is key in the NIATx model, whether it's between staff and change team members, change team leaders and NIATx coaches, or organizations. We facilitate this interactivity and network building in a variety of ways:

- Learning Collaboratives: During a learning collaborative, organizations come together to launch synchronized change projects. The members of the learning collaborative meet regularly along with a NIATx coach to learn about process improvement, and share their successes and challenges.

- Coaching: Organizations attempting change projects can receive individualized attention and guidance from a NIATx coach skilled in process improvement.

8

- Change Leader Academy: A special workshop for those interested in learning how to lead process improvement efforts.

- The NIATx website: Our website features a range of tools. We also host interactive forums and webinars on specific topics. (For more information, visit www.niatx.net)

The Business Case

As much as we focus on providing better care for clients, the financial side of running an agency can't be ignored. On the contrary, a strong financial footing provides the resources to offer quality care. A poor financial situation compromises the organization's ability to offer quality care and has a detrimental impact on working conditions and staff morale.

Improving the quality of care offered to your clients shouldn't mean sacrificing financial stability, and change projects that have a negative impact on finances are counterproductive to long-term improvement.

Because we understand these connections between care and business, we've made it a part of our mission to help organizations make changes that not only improve access and retention, but that also increase revenue and drive down costs. The NIATx model works because what is good for the clients is also good for the balance sheet. Our goals of getting more clients into treatment and keeping them there and maximizing efficiency and productivity align with putting the organization on surer financial footing[2].

9

NIATx Case Studies

Since NIATx began, we've worked with thousands of behavioral health treatment centers across the United States in a variety of ways—learning collaboratives, NIATx initiatives, coaching, conferences, and many others. Throughout this book, you'll find case studies from agencies that have used the NIATx model, and you'll learn about their experiences, their frustrations, what worked for them, and what didn't. We view every change project as a learning experience for the participants as well as other organizations. The NIATx website offers a growing inventory of success stories from organizations using the NIATx model to address a variety of issues—ranging from access to and retention in treatment to building their capacity to bill third-party payers.

How to Use this Book

This book is intended to provide both clear instruction and guidance on initiating a NIATx change project as well as to explain the background and key concepts that underlie the model. Agency leaders seeking to stage a process improvement project and anyone interested in learning about process improvement can use it as a guide.

We encourage you to read through the entire book before beginning your project to get a better sense of the context for each stage of the model, the preparation involved, and how the model works as a whole.

Chapter 1: Background

Founded in 2003, NIATx is still a relatively young program. However, process improvement, the theoretical foundation on which we built our model, can be traced back to the mid-20th century. Not so much methodology as an approach to achieving organizational goals, process improvement (and associated concepts like quality management) has, since it first emerged in the 1920s, been the basis for numerous theories, models, and methodologies put forth by both the pioneers of process improvement, like W. Edwards Deming and Joseph Juran, and more recent process improvement experts. Originally geared toward manufacturing, the process improvement approach has in recent decades been recognized as a powerful tool for enacting positive change in a number of fields outside the manufacturing sphere and has been applied to service industries since the 1980s.

Like all methods of process improvement, NIATx relies heavily on the work of Deming, who was born in 1900 and who is often referred to as "the father of process improvement." Deming's early work focused on applying statistics (his specialty) to quality control in manufacturing. Rather than rely on post-production inspections to weed out defective products, manufacturers should, Deming argued, build quality control into each step of design and production. In other words, instead of fixing a problem after it happens (by sorting out the defective goods), manufacturers should identify the process that allowed the defect to be created in the first place, and fix that. In doing so, they would create a higher-quality product while making production more efficient and cost effective.

(11)

Although a statistical approach to quality control was a focal point of Deming's work, his contribution to industrial management was not just a methodology, but also a larger philosophy of management. Instead of attempting to cuts costs wherever possible, often at the expense of quality, Deming argued that if manufacturers put a higher value on producing quality products, and paid close attention to quality at every step of the production process, they would not only produce a superior good[1] but would also streamline production.

Deming's platform for management set forth theories on how this kind of quality-driven infrastructure and culture might be developed. His holistic view of production examined each process in the context of the larger system in which it plays a part. Believing that the concept of quality only holds meaning in the context of customer needs, he posited that a business must predict and respond to customer needs during product design and development. He also advocated breaking down the antagonism that often existed between management and workers, encouraging collaboration rather than separation. He saw workers as an integral part of the system with a deep knowledge of their particular arena and valuable opinions.

Central to Deming's philosophy was the notion that improvement should be a continuous effort that builds upon itself, rather than finite change. In Deming's view, improvement should be cyclic, as designs are tested and refined in response to customer feedback and data, with input along the way from all who are involved with the system[2].

As the concept of process improvement took root in the 1980s, multiple management strategies, such as Six Sigma, emerged from it. It wasn't long before business leaders and scholars began to explore its potential for use outside the manufacturing sphere, including, notably, in the healthcare industry[3]. In the late 1980s, the National Project Demonstration for Quality Improvement in Healthcare established that healthcare could indeed benefit from process improvement[4], and in the 1990s, one of its directors, Donald Berwick, went on to found the Institute for Healthcare Improvement, an organization focused on strategically improving healthcare systems. By the end of the 1990s, convincing evidence of process improvement's potential to transform healthcare systems had emerged, but it had yet to be tested in the realm of substance abuse treatment.

The Origins of NIATx

In the years prior to the founding of NIATx in 2003, the substance abuse treatment field, like all areas of healthcare, was undergoing rapid change. New medications were being introduced, the financial landscape was changing; and within the field there was a growing recognition that addiction is, and should be treated as, a chronic condition, and that treatment delivery systems should be re-thought to reflect this reality.

In 2001, the Robert Wood Johnson Foundation (the Foundation) decided to move forward with a new initiative called Paths to Recovery. This project would approach the problem of improving treatment outcomes from a different direction. It had been established that the way in which treatment services are delivered has a significant impact on whether people with substance use disorders enter treatment and whether they stay long enough to benefit from it. Therefore, it stood to reason that the substance abuse treatment field could potentially benefit greatly from a methodology that used process improvement techniques to improve its business practices and work systems. The aim of the initiative was to develop a model for improving treatment outcomes by strategically redesigning work systems to function more efficiently and more effectively. Additionally, the initiative would establish an educational network of treatment centers, funding and providing technical assistance for improvement projects at each.

It was evident that the substance abuse treatment field had its own set of unique challenges when it comes to process improvement. Limited resources, high staff turnover, and a tendency to rely on conventional wisdom rather than empirical evidence could hamper organized improvement efforts. At the same time, these were the very challenges that process improvement had the potential to address. Furthermore, some of the field's central characteristics—a sense of purpose, dedication, and perseverance—would be assets in instituting a culture of continuous improvement, where it's key to be able to push through and keep going despite setbacks.

12

Victor Capoccia, a senior program officer at the Foundation, knew a bit about this from his experience as the CEO of CAB Health Services Inc., a not-for-profit substance abuse treatment and prevention center near Boston. After CAB's major growth during the 1990s, its leadership recognized the need to build an infrastructure that would both sustain this growth and promote additional progress. To that end, beginning in 1999, CAB carried out a project whose goal was to develop a work system that could support expanded and improved services. Dubbed "The Darwin Project" because of its focus on survival through evolution, this initiative showed that process improvement could be used successfully in the treatment field.

Paths to Recovery, though, would go further than the Darwin Project in that it was aimed at developing a standardized methodology to apply process improvement techniques in the substance abuse treatment setting. Additionally, the initiative would educate the field about process improvement, and fund and provide support for process improvement projects at selected treatment agencies. Recognizing that to develop an effective model of process improvement the initiative would need to narrow its focus, the Foundation decided that the targets of the model would be the issues of access to and retention in treatment, as these are widely recognized to be among the most pressing issues in the field.

Simultaneously, the federal government's Center for Substance Abuse Treatment (CSAT) was also considering how the treatment field might benefit from process improvement. It initiated a program called Strengthening Treatment Access and Retention (STAR), which, like Paths to Recovery, would fund systems-oriented improvement efforts at a number of treatment centers. Recognizing this common aim, the Foundation and CSAT decided to form a partnership, and the Network for the Improvement of Addiction Treatment (NIATx) was officially born. Dr. David Gustafson, director of the Center for Health Systems Research and Analysis at the University of Wisconsin–Madison was then chosen to direct the initiative. He brought with him decades of experience in improving healthcare systems.

Developing a Model
In addition to educating the field about process improvement, an important part of NIATx was to design an improvement model specifically for the substance abuse treatment field. It was essential to us that the model be as simple as possible, as unnecessary complexity could serve as a deterrent to change.

> The Five NIATx Principles
> 1. Understand and involve the customer
> 2. Fix key problems
> 3. Pick a powerful change leader
> 4. Get ideas from outside the organization or field
> 5. Use rapid-cycle testing

You'll note that the five principles of the NIATx model are closely tied with Deming's key points for management. Though Deming's platform related to manufacturing, the underlying principles— sensitivity to customer needs, paying attention to data, and an involved leadership—have value well beyond the manufacturing realm. These five principles provide the theoretical underpinnings for the NIATx model, and they also informed our development of the model from a procedural perspective. This is particularly true of the fifth principle— using rapid-cycle testing.

> In rapid-cycle testing, NIATx change teams conduct repeated PDSA (Plan-Do-Study-Act) Cycles to implement an idea on a small scale to see how it works. The team tests the change, modifies it, tests it again. PDSA Cycles continue until the change meets the targeted aim. Only then does it become a permanent change.

PDSA (Plan, Do, Study, Act) Cycles were the brainchild of Deming's mentor, Walter Shewhart, and Deming himself later built on them. They embody Deming's, and now our, conviction that improvement should be continuous and that innovations should be responsive to feedback, data, and newly-acquired knowledge. Thoughtful testing is the mechanism by which quality is built into the service design at each step of the way. It was also important to us, when we designed the model, that the testing process be as simple as possible. For that reason, we chose to put limits on the time devoted to each test, and encourage quick, easy methods for collecting data.

14

Preparing the Field

Although process improvement techniques had been employed with success in other healthcare arenas, it was a new concept for the substance abuse treatment field. Grants existed for specific treatment objectives, but there was no grant system that supported building better delivery systems for treatment. We recognized that we would need to prepare the field by engaging substance abuse treatment agencies and acquainting them with the concepts of process improvement.

We did this by staging a series of meetings all across the country that were attended by over 800 treatment professionals from all over the United States. In addition to introducing them to the initiative and to the concepts of process improvement, we used the conferences themselves to demonstrate to participants a better way to do things. By doing things like instituting simple registration systems for the conferences and staging greetings for participants, we modeled our conferences after the same principles we would be teaching. Through this, our participants were able to learn about process improvement, not just through the content introduced in the conferences, but also by the way the conferences themselves were set up. Additionally, we established a website (www.niatx.net) to provide additional information, news, and resources.

Assembling the Network

We knew that we would need to take great care in selecting which organizations would participate in the network. Our goal in crafting a call for proposals was not to attract as many organizations as possible, but to attract those organizations that demonstrated a firm commitment to change and that seemed most capable of seeing the project through successfully. In the first stage, we asked applicants to perform a walk-through of their admissions process and submit a letter of intent that identified strengths and weaknesses discovered in the walk-through.

We included the walk-through because we knew from personal experience how enlightening it can be. During his preparation to take on the role of NIATx national program office director, Dr. Gustafson had done a walk-through himself of the services at a local treatment agency, taking on the role of a heroin addict seeking treatment. The experience was illuminating. As Dr. Gustafson learned, the barriers that addicts face in accessing treatment, from unanswered phones to weeks-long waiting lists, can be overwhelming. In asking potential grantees to perform their own walk-throughs, we knew that they could attain a truer and more comprehensive understanding of the strengths and weaknesses of their organizations. The walk-through would also introduce them to the type of issues that the initiative would address.

From over 400 organizations that submitted letters of intent, we invited a smaller group to submit full proposals. Using the knowledge gained during the walk-through, each organization was asked to carry out a rapid-cycle change project that addressed one perceived problem.

(15)

Twenty-six organizations were eventually selected to participate in the network with funding from the Foundation's Paths to Recovery grant. Thirteen providers funded through and selected by CSAT's STAR program joined them.

Once the grantees had been selected, work began immediately. In keeping with our principle of looking to other industries for ideas, we staged a daylong meeting that connected our grantees with innovative thinkers from both inside the treatment field and outside it (such as the restaurant and airline industries) to identify promising solutions for increasing access and retention. Grantee organizations were also provided with a coach experienced in process improvement techniques to help guide and advise them in their projects. This type of personalized, hands-on coaching has become an integral part of our program.

From this beginning, with a few dozen treatment centers, NIATx has flourished and grown into a network of more than 2,500 providers, payers, and regulators in multiple fields including mental health, public health, criminal justice, and child welfare. In the spirit of continuous improvement, we've used the knowledge we gained from our first round of grantees, and every round since then, to strengthen our program even further and to share that knowledge with the field. Though our program has evolved as our experience and body of knowledge has grown, our philosophy remains rooted in the same principles that inspired the creation of NIATx. These principles have helped hundreds of organizations redesign their service delivery systems to reach more people and to offer better, more effective care.

Chapter 2: The Five Principles

As we've mentioned above, the NIATx model for process improvement centers on five essential principles. These five principles form the core of the NIATx philosophy, and they have been shown to play a critical role in the outcome of an improvement project.

> The five NIATx principles are:
> 1. Understand and Involve the Customer
> 2. Fix Key Problems
> 3. Pick a Powerful Change Leader
> 4. Get Ideas from Outside the Organization or Field
> 5. Use Rapid-Cycle Testing to Establish Effective Changes

Why do some improvement efforts succeed while others fail? What makes the difference? These questions underlie the NIATx model of process improvement. By understanding the essential elements of successful change, we can more effectively and efficiently improve the functioning of organizations.

Before we discuss the five principles in detail, we'll shed some light on their background—their origins, the evidence supporting them, and how they became the backbone of NIATx. We set out to learn which factors in an improvement effort made the difference between success and failure—in other words, which factors were responsible for whether a project failed or succeeded. To get this kind of information, we knew that we would need to compare successful organizational improvement projects and unsuccessful ones to identify patterns: which factors were present again and again in the successful projects, but were usually missing in unsuccessful ones? Conversely, which factors were present in the unsuccessful projects but not in the successful ones?

Fortunately, we discovered that a number of studies in the United States and abroad had already produced the type of data that we would need for our analysis. Different investigators conducted these studies at different times over the course of three decades, examining different firms and industries using different methodologies. However, in general, the studies we chose operated in a similar way: the investigators identified improvement or innovation projects that had been initiated by various firms in a particular industry or industries. Each of the projects chosen could be clearly categorized as either successful or unsuccessful. Then, relying on questionnaires and interviews with firm executives, the investigators measured the extent to which certain factors—principles, practices, or characteristics—had been present in each project. In all, the studies gathered data from 640 organizations in 13 industries, examining a total of 80 factors.

In brief, the studies that we reviewed were:

Project Sappho (and the related studies SAPPHO II and the Hungarian SAPPHO project): Project SAPPHO measured the presence of 122 variables in 72 pairs of innovations in the chemical and scientific instrument industries. Each pair consisted of one innovation that had been a categorical commercial success, and one that had not.

Stanford Innovation Project: The Stanford Innovation Project evaluated the characteristics of 59 pairs of innovations, one successful and one not for each pair, in the electronics industry.

Gerstenfeld Study: The Gerstenfeld study focused on innovations in the chemical, electrotechnical, and automotive industries, examining 11 successful innovations and 11 unsuccessful.

Project NewProd: Project NewProd measured the characteristics present in successful vs. unsuccessful new products put out by a total of 103 Canadian industrial goods firms in 13 industries.

Utterback Innovation Studies: The Utterback study evaluated 164 projects carried out by 59 firms in Europe and Asia in the computer, consumer electronics, automotive, chemical, and textile industries.

Delbecq and Mills: Delbecq and Mills studied the characteristics present in high-innovation firms vs. low-innovation firms (as opposed to specific projects, as in the other studies) in the high-tech and health services fields.

> Terminology: For our purposes, the terms "variables" and "factors" are synonymous; they both refer to the characteristics of a project that may or may not have influenced its outcome.

Despite the fact that these investigations differed in terms of the industries being studied and the methodologies used, they all had one very important thing in common: Each investigation measured the characteristics present not only in successful projects, but also the extent to which those characteristics were present in the unsuccessful projects under review. This was critical for our purposes, because it enabled us to determine not only which characteristics tended to be present in successful projects, but also whether those characteristics were usually present in unsuccessful projects, as well. In other words, it allowed us to identify which factors differentiated successful projects from unsuccessful, and thus which factors may be responsible for success.

Because different investigators undertook each study, the factors being evaluated varied from study to study. Since our analysis required us to find patterns across all the studies, we decided to group like with like: Factors that were labeled differently from study to study but that seemed to be describing essentially the same characteristics, or factors that seemed to be individual aspects of a larger umbrella category, were grouped together and evaluated as such.

Once we had identified and categorized the factors that we would be measuring, we crunched the numbers, using a ratio to express each variable's presence in successful projects vs. unsuccessful. The ratio illustrated the number of successful projects where this variable was present to the number of unsuccessful ones where the variable was present. So, for instance, if Variable X's ratio was 15:2, that would mean that for every 17 projects where variable X was present, 15 had been successful and 2 had been unsuccessful. If the first number was significantly higher than the second, we knew we might be on to something.

And what did we discover? As we had suspected, our analysis revealed commonalities and patterns across the studies. The conclusion we reached was remarkable: What we found was that out of the 80 variables examined, only five were statistically significant in differentiating between successful and failed projects. These five factors served as predictors of a project's outcome[1], and it was out of these five factors that the NIATx principles were born.

Let's look at the five NIATx principles:

Understand and Involve the Customer

There is a reason that we made this the Number One principle of NIATx. As it turned out, this single factor had more influence in whether a project was successful than all the other factors put together.

(19)

Its importance really can't be overstated. A company that takes the time and effort to get inside the head of its customer, to figure out his needs and to get regular feedback along the way, is far more likely to succeed in its improvement efforts. It's easy for a company to assume that it knows what its customers want, but to do so is a mistake. Throw any assumptions out the window and begin the project with the mindset that you don't know what the customer wants, or how she feels. When you start with a blank slate, you'll be forced to open up your eyes to the customer's point of view and to solicit and value customer input. The project will be much the better for it.

This point arises again and again in NIATx, and you'll likewise see it pop up again and again throughout this book; it's that important. One of the most valuable tools for seeing your organization through the customer's eyes is what we call "the walk-through." During the walk-through, which takes place at the beginning of a change project, you'll take on the role of a client seeking help from your agency. You will literally go through all the steps a typical client would go through, such as making the first phone call to inquire about services and actually filling out all the required paperwork during intake. In doing so, you can see your organization and its services the way a typical client does. You'll also be in a better position to identify problems and flaws that negatively affect customer perceptions. You'll find more information about the walk-through in Chapter 4.

Understanding the customer and customer needs is an ongoing process that doesn't end with one walk-through. Using repeated walk-throughs of many customer processes and gathering customer surveys, interviews, and focus groups, as well as getting staff input about what works for the customer and what doesn't, are all parts of understanding the customer and how your services work for him. With time, considering the client's point of view will no longer be a sporadic effort, but will become a constant habit ingrained into the culture of your organization.

Get Ideas from Outside the Organization or Field

Another significant predictor of success that we discovered in our review is the extent to which an organization looks to external sources for ideas or insights during a project. In the NIATx model, an organization attempting a process improvement project looks to the practices and standards of other industries, using creative thinking to identify processes and practices that could be adopted or adapted to their practice setting. What can you learn from the automotive industry? What about hotels? No matter how far removed two industries may seem, if you look hard enough you'll almost always be able to find commonalities: processes, practices, or challenges that, though situated in different contexts, are in some way similar or analogous. Searching for these threads promotes the kind of outside-the-box thinking that can yield ideas that would have never crossed your mind had you limited your brainstorming to familiar ground.

20

First, look for an example of a company that's the best at doing the thing that you are interested in improving. Then ask, "What makes that company so good?" For instance, let's say you are trying to set up a communication program in your organization. What other industries are great at communication? There are a lot of them, but one is the music industry. What organization stands out in the music industry as a particularly innovative one? Some might say Apple®. When you perform a search on the Internet for "What makes Apple® so good?" you'll find lots of analyses. One posits that Apple® goes out of its way to reward the creators of communications. They don't steal stuff, and they make sure it's a win–win strategy. How might that principle be adapted? One way would be to decide that no matter what communication system is developed, it must have a way to reward the creators of communications.

Use Rapid-Cycle Testing to Establish Effective Changes

As we reviewed the data we had compiled, it became clear that projects that tended to be successful were those that put a priority on developing a product of superior quality. In a successful project, development is efficient and effective, and the product is refined and perfected before it reaches the market, ensuring that flaws are eliminated and the customer receives a product that delivers exactly what he or she needs or wants.

You might wonder how that concept relates to process change in the behavioral health or other social services. We're not manufacturing a tangible product, after all. For our purposes, though, the concept still stands; in our case, the "product" being developed is the new and improved process itself. The product is the service that your organization provides. The way we refine and perfect our product is by quickly testing it, over and over, during the development stage, before implementing the newly designed service on a full scale.

In the NIATx model, potential changes that seem promising are put through the ringer before they're fully implemented. We want evidence that the change will yield an improvement toward the project's aim, and that the new process will work both for clients and the organization itself. And we want ideas on how to make it better at each cycle. To that end, it's essential that we have the opportunity to make adjustments as needed before the "product" is unveiled. As you'll see in Chapter 6, each potential change goes through a series of quick, rapid-succession pilot tests. During these tests, the change is implemented on a limited scale (on a handful of clients, say) for a short time (never longer than a couple weeks, and often far less). During each test, aim-related data are collected to determine whether the change is yielding an improvement. Then the team discusses how well the test went, and how the change might be modified to produce even better results. If the change yields promise, it's modified as needed and retested on a slightly larger scale; the cycle continues as many times as necessary.

> In rapid-cycle testing, NIATx change teams conduct repeated PDSA (Plan-Do-Study-Act) Cycles to implement an idea on a small scale to see how it works. The team tests the change, modifies it, tests it again. PDSA Cycles continue until the change meets the targeted aim. Only then does it become a permanent change.

(21)

By cycling through refining and testing and refining and testing, we can ensure that all the kinks and flaws have been worked out before the new process is implemented and that the product is of the highest possible quality—that it's as efficient as possible, that it delivers results with regard to the aim at hand, and that it improves the quality of care we provide for our clients.

Pick a Powerful Change leader

Our review showed us how important it is that a leader with strength and authority leads a project, and we've used this knowledge to inform our idea of what makes an ideal change leader. In the NIATx model, the executive sponsor of a change project selects one person to be the project leader—the change leader— to manage the change team and to supervise and direct the project. That person is held responsible for making the project a success. For a project to be successful, it needs to be led by someone who's respected by colleagues at every level of the organization and who can keep the agency's senior leadership interested in and committed to the project. The change leader should be someone who's comfortable calling the CEO at home at night to discuss the project, and who has the authority, power, and skills to do whatever it takes to keep moving the project forward. In Chapter 5, you'll learn about the specific responsibilities of the change leader and the qualities to look for when selecting who will lead a project.

Fix Key Problems

This principle flowed naturally from what we learned when we reviewed the role that organizational management plays in a project's outcome. What we found was that not only is it crucial that a respected, powerful, and authoritative change leader leads the project, but also that the project has the full support and backing of the organization's top management. Our investigation revealed that change projects are more likely to be successful when the top management is involved and committed to the project. This commitment means that the project will likely receive the support and resources needed for it to succeed.

That's where our principle of fixing key problems comes in or, as we often put it, fixing the problems that keep the CEO up at night. When you make improvements to problems that the CEO perceives to be important (which are often related to finances), chances are the CEO will remain committed to the project and to the whole concept of creating a culture of change within the organization.

We often hear the question, "How do you get CEO buy-in?" A better question might be "How does our project buy in to what the CEO is trying to accomplish? Is that relationship crystal clear to everyone involved?"

Another dimension to consider is how to keep CEO buy-in. One way is to get results quickly. The longer it takes to finish a project, the more likely other things of importance will pop up and take away senior leadership attention. Ideally a quality improvement project should be a hard-charging affair that can be completed in two or three weeks.

The case study that follows shows how one agency addressed a key problem that was keeping the CEO awake at night: how to increase revenue.

A Case Study: Fix Key Problems

About the Organization

Fayette Companies, based in Peoria, Illinois, provides mental health and substance abuse treatment services. Fayette Companies serves men, women, seniors, and adolescents regardless of their income across multiple levels of care.

Aim

• Increase continuation

Changes

The Fayette Companies change team did a walk-through of the admission process to one of its residential treatment programs for women. They found the process to be strict and unwelcoming and suspected that it was contributing to the discontinuation rate of 12.6 percent during the first week of treatment. Residential treatment is the most expensive level of care, and the high discontinuation rate was wasting resources.

The first change the team tested was to make the environment more welcoming. Family members were invited to participate in the admission process. A peer or staff member provided an orientation to the facility. Other changes included placing a moratorium on Friday admissions, since 47 % of those leaving in the first seven days of treatment were admitted on a Friday. Fayette staff recognized that it was harder to engage clients in treatment when they were admitted on a Friday.

23

Results

• In the first weeks of the changes, no women left during the first week of treatment. Occupancy increased from FY04 to FY05 by 921 days. The average length of stay increased by 11 days during this time period. Increased occupancy increased revenue by approximately $149,000.

• Sustaining the changes in FY06 also resulted in an increase in revenue of $224,000.

• The overall percentage of women leaving against medical advice at any point in treatment was reduced from almost 30 % at baseline to 11–12 % in subsequent years.

Fayette Companies learned that listening to customers is an essential part of the change process. They also learned that process improvement starts a chain reaction that inevitably results in better services, improved outcomes, and increased funding.

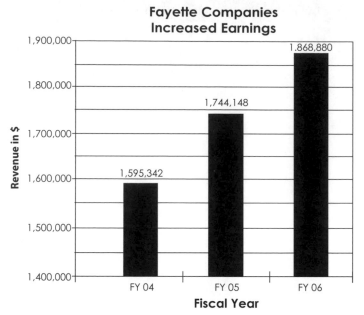

Fayette Companies Increased Earnings

Fayette Companies' change project increased continuation and revenue.

In Summary

The five principles of NIATx provide you a framework for process improvement projects that focus on the customer, have the endorsement of top management, are led by effective change leaders, seek ideas and inspiration from other organizations and fields, and rely on data to verify results.

Chapter 3: The NIATx Aims

Change projects in the NIATx mold are not open-ended endeavors meant to produce some vague, undefined notion of general improvement. On the contrary, they are focused, data-driven efforts whose objective is to produce a predetermined, measurable improvement in a particular arena.

When we began NIATx, we conceptualized four aims that would serve as the driving forces in our model for process improvement. These aims are straightforward, clearly defined, and easily measured outcomes that will truly make a difference in the quality of care that an organization provides and the efficiency of the system as a whole. In this chapter, we introduce you to the original four NIATx aims as well as additional aims that have since been included in the expanding NIATx program.

Why is it so important to define your aim? The short answer is that if you know what you're trying to do, you're more likely to produce a desirable outcome. Designing a change project around a specific aim ensures that the project remains focused and structured, and by choosing that aim wisely you know that the project is changing the system in ways that really matter. Remember the second NIATx principle of fixing key problems within the organization. It doesn't make much sense to put an enormous effort into a project that doesn't solve important problems or lead to important outcomes.

Additionally, having a clear objective allows for a framework for measuring progress. In a NIATx project, an organization decides in which area it wants to improve, evaluates its current performance level in that area, and sets a numeric goal for the performance level that it hopes to achieve through the change project. Throughout the change project, as changes are pilot tested, the change team is able to quantify progress with respect to that goal. In other words, the team gathers evidence as to whether a change is truly producing positive results.

And finally, approaching process improvement with a narrowly defined objective makes the project seem less daunting for those involved, and does in fact make the project more manageable. Process improvement is less overwhelming and less confusing when it's divided into discrete components.

NIATx Aims: The Original Four

Take a step back for a moment and think about the big-picture goals of your organization. It strives to aid clients' recovery from their illness, while maintaining a level of financial health that will allow the organization to continue to provide those services.

Now think about what is necessary to achieve that goal.

Recovering from addiction and mental illness is an enormous struggle, even under the best of circumstances. Treatment agencies should strive to create those "best" circumstances for recovery, rather than exacerbating the struggle with an ineffectual or inefficient delivery system. The goal of redesigning processes is to eliminate barriers to treatment, and do all we can to facilitate the clients' recovery.

What are the essentials for recovery? There are different types of services that may be delivered in different environments by different types of staff. The one absolute requirement, though, for an organization to help a client recover, is the client's presence. Your agency can't help someone who won't or can't get to your services or is so turned off by them that they come once and drop out. This is a huge problem for behavioral health agencies. Engaging and retaining clients is essential for successful recovery, yet it's where most agencies fall short. The inability to draw more people into treatment or to keep them there long enough to recover can seem like a problem inherent in the nature of the industry—we can blame the customer for lack of motivation or believe that it's a client's choice to reject services. In actuality, examining the infrastructure and processes of almost any treatment agency uncovers numerous processes and practices that act as barriers to clients' entering and remaining in treatment. This examination also reveals the absence of practices that could enhance the client's experience and increase engagement and retention.

It's for these reasons that we initially chose to focus the NIATx model on the problems of access (getting the client into treatment) and retention (keeping the client in treatment). We based our decision on research from the Washington Circle, a group of policy makers, providers, researchers, and managed-care representatives that was convened to develop and pilot test measures for evaluating the performance of substance-abuse treatment agencies. The Washington Circle has pilot-tested and adopted three core performance measures— identification, initiation, and engagement—that have been adopted by the National Quality Forum and the National Committee on Quality Assurance as consensus standards. We developed measures for these standards that were easy to capture and clear in their definition. Since identification is frequently done outside the treatment system, we focused on initiation and engagement, or access to and retention in treatment.

Increasing Access to Treatment

NIATx Aim: Reducing Waiting Time. "Waiting time" refers to the average amount of time a client must wait between her first request for treatment and her first session. Long waiting periods for services are a recurring problem in behavioral health, and they are detrimental to recovery. The longer a client waits to get services, the more opportunity there is for him to lose interest, get cold feet, or forget the appointment. Many organizations have long waiting periods simply because of inefficient processes; change projects addressing the process aim work to identify these inefficiencies and eliminate them.

NIATx Aim: Increasing Admissions. It goes without saying that entering treatment is the first step to recovery. Increasing admissions means you are helping more people and, because you're doing it using existing resources, you're also improving the agency's bottom line.

Increasing the number of admitted clients can be a matter of increasing the number of referrals to the agency, increasing the number of referred clients who end up admitted or, in the case of an agency that is already booked full, increasing capacity (i.e., increasing the number of clients the agency can treat at any given time) by redesigning the existing system to be more efficient.

Case Study: Reduce Wait Time

About the Organization

Prestera Center for Mental Health Services serves an eight-county region in West Virginia, providing mental health and substance abuse services to both children and adults. Prestera's 49 sites feature a range of services, including 24-hour emergency care, outpatient, detoxification, public inebriate services, and residential substance abuse treatment, both long- and short-term.

Aim

• Reduce waiting time for outpatient mental health treatment

Changes

To monitor the effectiveness of the changes they were testing, the Route 60 Change Team decided to measure time from first contact to first therapy, number of no-shows, and number of admissions.

The first change the Prestera team tested was to revise its intake scheduling. They decided to eliminate the multiple visits previously required before a client could even begin therapy. The change the team tested was to offer 12 available intake appointments every day, with six slots each either in the morning or the afternoon.

Along with that, the change team worked to standardize the intake appointment process. The walk-through revealed that completing an intake could take from 20 minutes to more than two hours. They set a goal to reduce that to no more than 90 minutes.

Results

Streamlining and standardizing the intake process allowed the intake worker to offer the client a brief 15-minute therapy orientation with a therapist that same day. If a patient chose not to meet with a therapist on the same day, the intake worker would then offer the next available therapy appointment. With the revised scheduling, most clients could see a therapist within two weeks of their intake appointment.

• As a result of this change project, waiting time for outpatient mental health services dropped from 37.66 days pre change to 19.77 days—a reduction of about 48 percent.

- Reduced times to treatment increased the number of clients scheduled for therapy.

- Reduced waiting times also increased revenue from completed intake appointments.

- Another pleasant surprise for the team was seeing data in a new way. While they were accustomed to sharing data, usually they found that the reports and statistics available were too old to be relevant. A weekly review of data showing steady improvement in reducing waiting times was new and refreshing for the team.

- With the change in scheduling to accommodate same-day or next-day intake appointments, intake staff could not keep up with phone calls. To address this challenge, a staff person from another area was assigned to answer calls during the same-day intake periods.

- The improved intake appointment scheduling process maximized therapist time, and therapists were able to accommodate additional appointments.

Increasing Retention in Treatment

NIATx Aim: Reduce No-Shows. A no-show is when a client fails to show up for a scheduled appointment, and an agency's no-show rate can be calculated by dividing the number of no-shows by the total number of scheduled appointments. When clients miss appointments, it can derail their treatment, waste valuable counselor and staff time, and act as a barrier to treatment for other clients who could have used that wasted time slot. Reducing no-shows to appointments (including assessments) means that more clients are getting treatment and that the organization's time is being used more efficiently.

The reasons that clients miss appointments usually fall into one of two categories: logistical barriers (for example, the client has no means of getting to the facility) or mental/emotional barriers (such as when a client is frightened of or ambivalent about the prospect of treatment). Change projects addressing this aim have addressed both of these categories.

NIATx Aim: Increase Continuation. Specifically, we aim to increase the percentage of clients who remain in treatment through the fourth treatment session. The reason the fourth treatment session has been used is that it easy to measure in a short time frame and there is evidence that dropout rates decrease dramatically after the fourth session. Most people actually drop out between intake/assessment and their first appointment, so it's also a good idea to measure the percent of people who make it to their first session after assessment.

Dropouts are a major problem in behavioral health, as in many service settings where multiple appointments are the norm. A NIATx change project that is aimed at increasing continuation identifies the reasons that a client might drop out of treatment and then redesigns the processes in question so that those "reasons" are eliminated.

A Case Study: Reduce No-shows

About the organization

Located in Wooster, Massachusetts, AdCare provides inpatient detoxification and rehabilitation, outpatient detoxification, day treatment programs, intensive outpatient treatment, and individual, family, and group counseling. AdCare helps individuals and their families overcome the disease of addiction one life at a time.

Aim

• Reduce no-shows

Changes

The AdCare change team created a system for tracking clients who didn't show up for their first scheduled treatment session. Staff were trained to monitor the system. An assessor was assigned to make calls to no-show clients within 72 hours after the missed treatment session.

Results

• As a result of this change, AdCare was able to re-engage 75 percent of the clients who failed to show for their first appointment.

• No-shows through the first four treatment sessions decreased.

• This change generated an estimated 2,535 additional units of service in a three-month period (intensive outpatient, individual, or group sessions), representing a 20 percent increase in gross revenue.

By conducting this change project, the AdCare team learned that process improvement is ongoing, not a single event. They also recognized that while not all change projects are equally successful, they all support the overarching goal of improving client satisfaction.

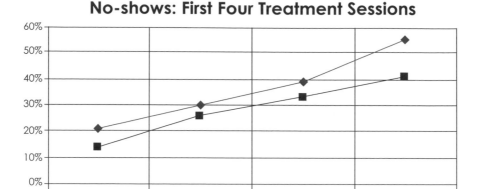

AdCare's change project reduced no-shows and increased revenue

The Bottom Line

Let's go back for a moment to the other part of the big-picture aim of behavioral health and social service agencies: maintaining the organization's financial health. At NIATx, we know that the financial health of an organization weighs heavily on the mind of its leadership, and is often the driving force behind key decisions. Furthermore, we know that it's difficult for change projects to succeed without the full backing and support of the organization's upper management. With that in mind, the NIATx aims were developed to not only improve the quality of care that an organization offers, but in doing so, to simultaneously improve the bottom line. Successful change projects make the treatment delivery system as efficient as possible, increasing revenue and eliminating unnecessary expenditures.

Choosing an Aim

Each NIATx aim needs and deserves its own dedicated change project because it's important to focus. Sometimes it will be clear which aim you need to prioritize. If you're unsure of where to start, perform an agency walk-through, as described in Chapter 5, to determine where problems lie and to prioritize them. As you do the walk-through, make notes of flaws, inefficiencies, or other problems that you, thinking as the client, notice or that staff members mention. Then think about which of the aims each problem might relate to: for example, if you, as the client, are told that the next available appointment isn't for two weeks, you might think about a project that addresses the waiting period. If you are put off by the physical environment or concerned about privacy during the initial visit, or you feel that you have received inadequate information about the treatment process, those might be indicators that real clients are failing to enter treatment for similar reasons.

If there are no clear priorities or specific areas of concern, we recommend tackling the four aims in this order:

- Reduce Waiting Times
- Reduce No-Shows
- Increase Continuation
- Increase Admissions

We settled on this order because, as you'll see when you get further into process improvement projects, these aims are not completely independent of one another. In fact, each is inextricably linked to the others. If you significantly reduce waiting times between the first contact and the first treatment session, you'll probably find an increase in the percentage of clients who actually show up for that first treatment session. Reducing no-shows logically increases continuation. If you decrease wait time and increase continuation, then you will increase the number of people whom you serve. Accomplishing the first three aims makes the treatment system more efficient, which can increase your organization's capacity and increase admissions. This interconnectedness is one of the reasons it's important to take the aims one at a time; otherwise the project might become unmanageably complex.

The NIATx Aims and the Treatment Continuum

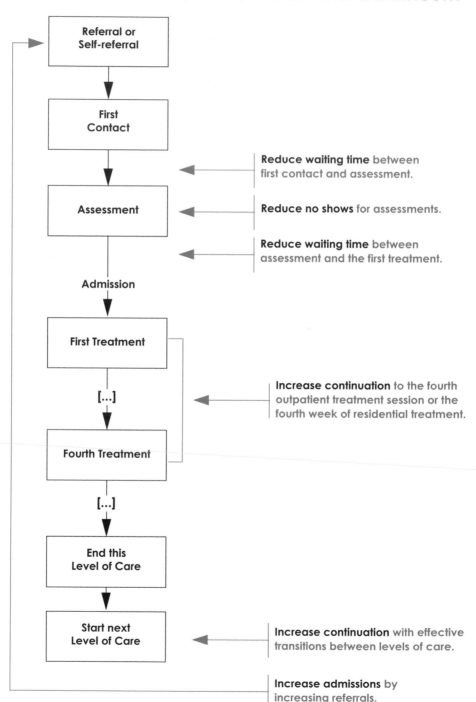

Expanding the NIATx Aims

As NIATx has moved forward, we've recognized other problems within the field that the NIATx model can address successfully, and we've begun projects to expand upon the original four aims. So far, we've added three additional aims to our catalogue:

- Improving handoffs (a client's transition between levels of care)
- Increasing the use of evidence-based practices in substance abuse treatment settings
- Improving back-office practices

Handoffs

One area in the treatment continuum that often proves to be problematic is the system by which a client is transferred between levels of care. We call this the "handoff," and it's not easy, but it's important. Any number of things that may go wrong during the handoff can be disruptive to the client's treatment and can be a major contributing factor to dropouts. In this sense, the handoff process is part of the NIATx aim of increasing continuation. However, because it's such a complex activity, and because it's so often handled poorly, it's deserving of its own focus and change project.

We decided to focus on improving handoffs because we recognized the need for a more systematic and seamless procedure for transferring clients between levels of care. Handoffs are challenging because there are so many opportunities for error: an abrupt transition can unnerve the client; crucial information can be communicated poorly or not communicated at all; if the transition is not seamless, clients may be lost in the gap between levels of care; the receiving level of care may not be sufficiently prepared for the particular needs of the client; a lack of synchronization between the two levels of care can make the transition chaotic and stressful; if there is no follow up, the client might not make it to the first appointment at the next level of care and no one would notice; the list goes on. Any one of these problems can mean the difference between a client's progressing in treatment or dropping out or relapsing.

33

In light of the handoff's importance and the potential for error, it's crucial that both the "delivering" team and the "receiving" team make a strong commitment to improving the system and to taking responsibility for the clients. It should never be considered the client's fault that he or she didn't make it to the next step. Remember that the system is designed to produce exactly the outcome that it produces. If 50 percent of people do not make it to the next level of care, then it's the problem of the handoff system, and the process between the deliverer and receiver must be changed.

Think about a system outside the treatment field where handoffs are smooth and efficient. Maybe it's the pit crew of a champion in a NASCAR race or the passing of a baton between Olympic relay racers. What makes them so good? How can you learn what makes them so good and use those ideas in client care transitions?

In the NIATx model, an organization attempting to improve its handoffs must look at the process not just as the moment that the client moves to the next level of care, but as the preparation for that moment conducted by the "delivering" and the "receiving" teams, and how those teams help the client make the transition to the next level of care. The goal is to standardize a perfected handoff procedure that results in consistently successful transitions.

Strong handoff systems rely on scripted, standardized methods of communication and face-to-face interaction between staff at both levels of care. This ensures that no vital information is omitted and provides an opportunity for questions and clarifications. The successful handoff system requires not only a coordinated system of communication between the delivering and receiving teams; it also requires significant preparation on both sides. The delivering team must ensure that all the correct information about the client is communicated to the receiving team, and they must also prepare the client for what lies ahead. The client should know what she can expect in the next level of care. The receiving team, for its part, must use the information imparted by the delivering team in advance of the client's arrival to adequately prepare, and should likewise make an effort to reassure the client.

The transition between levels of care should feel seamless for the client, which is why it's important to build bridges between the levels of care. Gaps in treatment are the enemies of recovery. To that end, handoffs change projects often experiment with overlapping the two levels of care by having the client meet with her counselor from the "receiving" level, or attend a meeting prior to making the transition.

Like any NIATx change project, improving the system of handoffs is about continuous evaluation and continuous improvement. Rather than get complacent after instituting a successful handoff system, the organization should keep asking how it could be made even better, with the knowledge that there is always room for more improvement.

A Case Study: Handoffs

About the Organization

Founded in 1970, Palladia, Inc., is today one of the largest not-for-profit, multiservice agencies in New York City. Palladia mainly works with poor, urban individuals and families of color. Palladia currently serves about 1,300 people per day in 24 programs, including two residential substance abuse treatment programs, four outpatient and transitional treatment programs, an HIV services unit, and one homeless and two domestic violence shelters.

The Starhill residential drug treatment program serves nearly 400 adult men and women in four separate Modified Therapeutic Community Programs at one site. All four programs use interdisciplinary treatment teams. Clients' length of stay varies from 6 to 12 months. Starhill residents follow a structured program that emphasizes personal accountability. The program's goal is to help the client's move from drug dependence and abuse to good health and sobriety.

Palladia's Continuing Care Treatment (CCT) offers outpatient aftercare services to clients who have graduated from Starhill and Palladia's other residential substance abuse treatment programs. CCT's services include individual and group addiction counseling and support, relapse prevention, vocational and educational services, job search assistance, and help with budgeting and housing. Although clients left Starhill with a referral to Continuing Care Treatment (CCT), many did not successfully transfer to CCT.

Aim
Create a seamless transition from residential to continuing care for each Starhill client.

Changes
The change team's walk-through made it clear that clients needed more education about continuing care and its role in continuing recovery. Some clients assumed that because they received a certificate of completion at the end of their residential stay, they no longer needed any treatment.

The walk-through also revealed that:

(35)

- Paperwork between the two facilities was frequently lost or delayed.

- CCT staff were not fully prepared to meet the needs of clients who did appear for continuing care.

- Frequent staff turnover al the CCT site inhibited the success of the program.

Through flow-charting, the team identified weaknesses in the Starhill discharge process and the CCT intake process. With a better picture of the discharge and intake process, the team was able to test modifications to the system. These included:

- Sending a patient's Starhill discharge application to CCT 30 days before the client's scheduled discharge date

- Testing the electronic transfer of paperwork between facilities

- Requiring CCT to call Starhill upon receiving the discharge paperwork and, within seven days of receiving it, schedule the client's CCT intake

- Requiring that Starhill clients complete CCT intake and attend at least two group sessions at CCT before leaving Starhill.

Results

Client response to the changes was positive. To address Starhill residents' need for more information about CCT, Starhill staff began to distribute information about the program, CCT staff offered monthly presentations about CCT at Starhill. These information services corrected many of the misconceptions that Starhill residents had previously had.

Evidence-based Practices

In 2006, NIATx began an initiative called Advancing Recovery, with the goal of creating partnerships between state purchasers of treatment services and the treatment providers. The purpose of these partnerships was to promote the use of evidence-based practices in the substance abuse treatment setting. Implementing evidence-based practices has become a new aim for NIATx process improvement projects.

Evidence-based practices are clinical practices that have been proven in some way to improve treatment outcomes, such as the use of medications for specific diagnoses. The practices we choose to focus on are ones that have the most evidence behind them through multiple clinical trials.

We approach the implementation of evidence-based practices much as we approach the original four aims, with the assumption that within the infrastructure of a treatment organization there are various processes and practices that act as barriers to the implementation of evidence-based practices (EBPs). A NIATx project aimed at implementing an EBP seeks to identify these barriers and test changes that will remove them and facilitate the new practice. Implementing EBPs may seem impossible for an organization, but through a change project the organization figures out why it seems so impossible and redesigns those parts of the system that stand in the way.

Just as in any NIATx change project, once these barriers have been identified, the change team brainstorms potential solutions and pilot-tests them, refining and retesting as necessary.

We emphasize the necessity of removing barriers to the implementation of a particular evidence-based practice because a new practice that is simply forced into the existing system is unlikely to be sustained. It's easy enough to instruct staff to begin implementing a particular practice, but unless the systemic organizational barriers inhibiting the standardization of the practice are removed through system redesigns, the new practice won't last long. Instead, we rebuild processes to accommodate the practice, which allows for both sustainability and for a well-functioning system.

A Case Study: Evidence-Based Practices

About the organization
For decades, Baltimore has had one of the highest rates of heroin addiction in the nation. The Baltimore Buprenorphine Initiative (BBI) brings together substance abuse treatment centers, community health centers, and primary care physicians to combat this problem in Baltimore City.

Launched in February 2008 as part of the BBI, Baltimore's Advancing Recovery project sought to remove barriers to the use of medication-assisted treatment—an evidence-based practice–and improve continuing care among patients, both at the treatment program and in physician offices in the community.

Treatment includes dose induction, stabilization, and continuation on buprenorphine combined with intensive outpatient counseling (IOP). Following IOP, patients receive extended buprenorphine therapy. The participating providers transfer stabilized patients with pharmacy and healthcare benefits to physicians in community health centers and other settings.

Aim
• Reduce waiting time

• Increase use of evidence-based practice (medication-assisted treatment)

Changes
A walk-though of the provider intake process revealed that the process needed to be more manageable for patients, counselors, and administrative staff. Improving the intake process would help the BBI achieve its first aim, reducing waiting time, both from first request to first face-to-face contact and from first face-to-face contact to first medication dose.

The first change the team tested to improve the intake process was to shift the focus from paper work and funding regulations to engaging patients in treatment. One agency was able to reduce 19 forms requiring patient signatures witnessed by a counselor to a single form.

Results
The project reduced both types of waiting time, and patient response to the changes was positive. As one change team member put it "Patients can now get the medication on the same day or the next day, where they used to have to wait three weeks. Patients say that buprenorphine has changed their lives—now they can work and take care of their children."

Reduced waiting time did not have the expected positive impact on patients' continuation in treatment. To improve the IOP retention rate, the change team applied the NIATx principle, "understand and involve the customer," by holding six patient focus groups. Participating patients had various lengths of stay in treatment. The focus groups were held at provider sites. An independent facilitator conducted the groups. In addition, every patient appearing for treatment during a two-day period at each provider site was asked to complete a paper survey about his or her treatment needs. Telephone surveys of patients who had dropped out of treatment were also conducted.

Through these efforts, the team learned that patients thought IOP required too great a time commitment. They also raised transportation and childcare issues as barriers to continuing treatment. Because of the limited number of buprenorphine "slots" in the city, patients sometimes had to travel long distances to receive the medication.

The focus groups also revealed that patients were more interested in individual counseling and help with housing and job skills than the educational content traditionally offered. As a result, BBI began to explore how to develop the requested services and counseling.

Patient input has been key in identifying barriers and how to remove them. "We're learning that we need consumer input all along the way and that we can refocus our efforts depending on what feedback we get from patients," said one change team member.

Improving Back Office Practices

Even if it provides great service to clients, an agency can lose money if its back office is not functioning as well as the front office or customer interactions. Many agencies struggle with financial management, particularly their billing process. The NIATx model has been applied to aims of increasing collections, reducing time in receivables, increasing timeliness of reporting, or other critical financial functions that meet the NIATx principle of solving key problems.

A Case Study: Improving Collections

About the organization

STEPS (Substance Abuse, Treatment, Education and Prevention Service) is a private, nonprofit organization dedicated to preventing and treating substance abuse. Located in Wooster, Ohio, STEPS is the largest treatment provider in Wayne and Holmes counties. STEPS has grown from a one-person office in 1974 to a 40-person organization providing a full continuum of care for individuals and their families. STEPS has been recognized within Ohio, and nationwide for innovation in administrative design and community service.

Aim

• Improve collections from third-party payers

Changes

STEPs created the "Insurance Bounty Hunters" change team. Two members of the team sought assistance from financial staff at another local treatment provider agency that had faced similar problems with reimbursements from insurance companies. The STEPS change team members explored state and insurance company requirements that had affected STEPS collection rates. For example, they learned that one reason for denials and poor collections was they had not been submitting claims on the required forms. They also realized that STEPS had been submitting claims for services provided by clinicians who were not properly credentialled.

The STEPS team then conducted a series of changes, which included:

• Building personal relationships with insurance company representatives. STEPS staff could contact the same person at the insurance company with questions about a denial and to thank that person for help in resolving a claim issue.

• Using the required Healthcare Financing Administration (HCFA) forms for submitting new claims and processing older unpaid claims.

• Making follow-up calls whenever a claim was rejected. This allowed STEPS staff to correct errors and resolve claim denials.

Results

By increasing attention to the billing process through understanding the insurer, developing relationships, and addressing all unpaid claims STEPS increased their revenue from third-party payers. The Insurance Bounty Hunters Change Team helped increase receipts from $500 per month to $6,000-9,000 per month.

In Summary

The NIATX aims can help to really focus your change efforts. While you may be ready to jump in and get started on a change project that targets all the aims, our model is based on focusing on one aim at a time, making a small change, measuring the impact of the change, and then making another change.

40

Chapter 4: The Walk-through

I n the NIATx model, the first phase in a change project is a procedure called the walk-through. During the walk-through, staff involved in the project take on the role of "customer" to experience the services offered by their organization exactly as a customer would, from the first phone call for help, through services, to the eventual discharge. In this section, we explain the purpose of the walk-through and offer detailed guidelines for how to go about conducting a walk-through.

The Purpose of the Walk-through

The walk-through is an essential component of the NIATx model because it allows you to see your organization from the customer's point of view. In doing so, you will gain a more comprehensive understanding about which of your agency's processes work well for the customer, and which ones need improvement.

Understanding and involving the customer is the first and most important of the NIATx principles, and the walk-through is the most crucial tool for accomplishing this. Of the five NIATx principles, understanding and involving the customer has been shown to have the greatest predictive power in determining which organizations will be successful in their change efforts. The insight you will gain from the walk-through will allow you to identify problematic practices in your organization and decide which aim or aims should be prioritized. From there, you can test solutions to these problems that will better serve the customer, the staff, and the financial bottom line.

People seeking behavioral health or social services are in a sensitive position. They may even not believe they need any help. They may be ambivalent or feel intimidated or frightened by the notion of treatment, and may therefore be easily discouraged by any bumps in the process. In fact, 50 percent of people seeking treatment never make it to their first appointment. Therefore, to enact positive changes that matter—changes that facilitate the client's access to and completion of treatment—you must first understand the unique concerns, feelings, and needs of your customers.

Each of the four NIATx aims—reducing waiting times, reducing no-shows, increasing admissions, and increasing continuation rates—are closely tied to the customer's perception of your agency. Small details of the treatment process can negatively affect this perception and subtly discourage the customer from entering and completing treatment. When you conduct the walk-through, you'll put yourself in the mindset of a customer. This will allow you to identify which processes facilitate the customer's smooth entry into and completion of services, and which ones make the experience more difficult for the customer, emotionally or logistically, and thus act as barriers to the successful completion of treatment.

Oftentimes, it's the details that make a big impact on the customer's perception of your agency. Many details that leave a negative impression on the customer can be improved at

41

little or no cost to the agency. For example, a customer may be overwhelmed by the amount of paperwork required; in that case, streamlining the required paperwork could increase the organization's admissions. Playing the role of customer and going through the treatment process as a customer would allow you to identify these negative details that might have otherwise been overlooked, and thus locate low-cost solutions that will make a positive impact on the customer's view of your agency.

It's easy for the management and staff of a treatment agency to make assumptions about the ways in which services are being delivered, but these assumptions often do not reflect reality. Policies and practices that should work in theory are sometimes less successful in practice, and oftentimes it takes an "outside" perspective to recognize this. By conducting the walk-through and taking on the role of customer, you'll be in a better position to locate procedural flaws and inefficiencies in the system.

Once you have completed the walk-through, the change team will be armed with a better understanding of which practices in the system stand in the way of customer access to and continuation of services. From there, you will be able to decide which areas of treatment need the most improvement, and which problems specifically need to be addressed.

How to Conduct a Walk-through

During the walk-through, you will take on the role of a customer seeking services with your organization and you will experience the treatment services your organization offers exactly as a customer would. This means that you will follow every procedure that a typical client would, from first contact through to eventual discharge. Note that it isn't necessary to walk through all of your organization's services in one go; it's fine to perform separate walk-throughs for different stages in the treatment continuum (for example, you might conduct a walk-through that focuses solely on the admissions process).

This is not a theoretical exercise; the point is not to "think through" your organization's treatment processes, but rather to actually physically and emotionally experience them. It's by actually going through the motions as a customer would that you'll notice the problematic details that might otherwise go unnoticed. For example, one agency discovered in the course of the walk-through that the phone number listed for the organization in the phone book was in fact not connected to a telephone at the organization. Who knows when this problem would have been discovered had they not literally gone through the motions of looking up and dialing the clinic number during the walk-through instead of just assuming that the number worked?

For this reason, you should not assume that any part of the process works without actually testing it out yourself during the walk-through. Try to find information about your agency in the way that a client might. If you perform an Internet search for addiction treatment in your community, for example, does your agency show up on the first page? You should call your organization to make an appointment or to get information; you should go through the initial assessment, filling out any paperwork and taking any tests that a typical customer would; and you should go through the treatment process, including transferring between levels of care. During each step of the walk-through process, you'll record your thoughts and feelings about which aspects of care you, thinking as a client, respond to negatively or positively.

You'll also ask the staff members involved in each step of the treatment process for their input about which aspects of care are problematic, and how those aspects could be improved. A walk-through is not mystery shopping. The purpose is not to catch staff doing something wrong, but to identify what aspects of the process need to be changed. Remember that processes, not the people doing them, cause 85 percent of customer problems. So step out of the role and ask staff questions about why they do something a certain way, how real clients react, and what their thoughts are on how to improve the process.

Once you have conducted the walk-through, you will use your notes on the experience to determine which areas of your organization need the most help and should thus be prioritized.

Now that you understand the purpose of the walk-through and have a general idea about how it works, you can use a form like the "Walk-through Recording Template" to plan the walk-through, do the walk-through, and study and act on your findings (PDSA Cycle). We've included a copy of the form on the pages that follow. You can also download this form and others from the Forms and Templates page of the NIATx website at www.niatx.net.

The more thought you put into planning the walk-through, the more you will get out of it.

43

Walk-through Recording Template

Use this template to record your experiences and observations from your walk-through exercise, as well as the suggestions that you've gathered from your staff.

Agency Name: | Enter your agency's name here... |

First Contact

Observations:	1. Did you get a busy signal, voice mail, an automated greeting, or did a live person answer the call?
	2. Did the agency offer you an appointment on your first call?
	3. How long did you wait for your first appointment?
	4. Would you have to miss work to attend the appointment?
	5. Would you have difficulty reaching the site without access to a car?
	6. Does the agency offer transportation to the site if you don't have transportation?
Recommendations:	

44

Visit the NIATx.net Resource Center "Forms and Templates" section to download this form.

Walk-through Recording Template

First Appointment

Observations:	1. Was it easy to find the agency?
	2. Were parking, directions, and signage adequate?
	3. Did the site feel pleasant and welcoming or cold and harsh?
	4. Were you welcomed to the agency in an open and friendly manner?
Recommendations:	

Intake and Assessment

Observations:	1. Did the family member accompany you through the entire intake process?
	2. How long did you spend in the waiting room?
	3. Was a urine test required?
	4. What was the assessment process like?
	5. Did you have to wait between your assessment and your first treatment session, and if so, how long?
Recommendations:	

45

Visit the NIATx.net Resource Center "Forms and Templates" section to download this form.

Walk-through Recording Template

First Treatment Session

Observations:	1. How were you treated?
	2. Did the agency contact you to confirm your treatment appointment?
	3. Was it clear where you were to go and what you could expect to happen?
	4. What questions or concerns should have been addressed before the first session?
Recommendations:	

Final Considerations

1. What surprised you most during your walk-through?

2. What changes do you most want to make?

Visit the NIATx.net Resource Center "Forms and Templates" section to download this form.

PLAN the Walk-through: Choose Who and When

The first step is to decide when to do the walk-through, and who should participate. There is a certain degree of flexibility in making these decisions, based on what makes the most sense for your particular organization. In some cases, the executive sponsor will conduct the walk-through herself before choosing the change leader and the change team. Alternatively, the walk-through can be conducted after the change leader and the change team have been selected. In some cases, the executive sponsor will have decided prior to the walk-through which of the NIATx aims he would like the team to address first; in other cases, the sponsor, leader, and team may use the results of the walk-through to decide which aim to address. Any of these options are acceptable; what matters most is which of them will suit the needs of your particular organization.

The number of people participating in the walk-through is also flexible; it can be just one person, or three people or more. However, we recommend that at least one person from upper management participate in the walk-through (ideally the CEO). It can also be helpful for a pair of people to conduct the walk-through together, with one person playing the role of the client seeking treatment, and the other person playing the role of the client's family member. This is the model that we use in explaining how to do the walk-through. Conducting the walk-through in pairs works well because it affords you more than one perspective on the experience, and it allows you to discuss the experience with a colleague.

It's a good idea to have a nonclinical person participate in the walk-through, either as the client or a family member. Clinical staff may be so used to the language or so embedded in the process that nothing will seem wrong even when the process is burdensome and difficult.

When deciding who will participate in a walk-through, be sure to choose people who are detail oriented and who are committed to getting the most out of the experience.

Create a Back Story

The next step is to create a background for the role you will be playing by deciding what problem you are seeking treatment for. It's important to choose something that you are familiar with, because you likely have a better understanding of the potential answers to the many questions you will be asked.

Inform the Staff

Finally, be sure to inform the affected staff ahead of time that you'll be conducting a walk-through. This is not meant to be a secretive exercise, and it's important that the staff not feel undermined. Reassure them that the purpose of the walk-through is to evaluate administrative and organizational processes, not the staff themselves.

Make a particular point to ask the staff to treat you as they would a typical customer. The walk-through will still be effective even if the staff are on their best behavior, because you are trying to capture issues with the process itself—you're not trying to catch staff doing something wrong.

Some things to keep in mind throughout the walk-through

- Only break character to ask questions or obtain additional information. Don't step into the supervisory or boss role and tell staff that they are doing something wrong. You are the client, family member, or occasionally the administrator trying to understand the process, not the boss doing staff oversight!

- Make a conscious effort to get into the mindset of a typical customer to experience your organization's facilities and treatments as if encountering them for the first time, the way a customer would. For example, would a non-clinician understand the language being used?

- If you've already been assigned to address a particular aim prior to the walk-through, pay extra attention to the processes that relate to the assigned aim.

- Be aware that a customer likely would have little or no knowledge of the treatment process and treatment terminology. When speaking with staff, ask yourself whether their descriptions of various steps in the treatment process would be accessible to customers unfamiliar with the services you deliver, or whether they might sound confusing.

- At each step in the walk-through, ask the staff members with whom you interact for their opinions and ideas about what works well and what doesn't. Staff members know the processes in question inside and out, and they likely have valuable ideas on what needs to be improved.

- Take notes! Write down your experiences at each step of the walk-through, including not just details about the processes themselves, but also about your emotional response to them. Write down the input you get from staff members, as well. If you are working with another person playing the role of family member, he should also take copious notes on the experience.

DO the Walk-through

Now that you've carefully planned the walk-through, you are ready to begin. Here we describe the four possible steps that you'll go through during your walk-through experience (first contact, the first appointment, the intake process, and transferring between levels of care) and how to get the most out of them in the walk-through. Throughout the walk-through, you should record your observations, making a note of which aspects of service worked well, and which ones were more negative. Remember to put yourself in the emotional mindset of someone who's seeking help and gauge your emotional response to each aspect of the interaction. In addition, keep an eye out for inefficiencies, such as redundant paperwork or processes that could be streamlined. Throughout the walk-through, ask the staff members you encounter for their thoughts about which processes don't seem as successful as they should be, and if they have any ideas for improvements that could make the experience more positive for the client, the client's family, and the staff. Be sure to take notes on the staff's opinions and ideas as well as your own.

Step One: First Contact

Before you even pick up the phone to contact your agency, ask yourself an important question: How would a potential customer know about your organization in the first place? Think about the typical places a potential customer might look for information about treatment (for example, the phone book or an Internet search) and test them out to see if your agency (and all the relevant information about your services) would come up in the potential client's search.

Then, make contact with your organization to schedule an appointment. To do this, you'll need to find the correct phone number. Remember, even though you likely know the phone number by heart, a typical client would have to look it up. Therefore, so should you. Once you've located the number, call it and if you reach someone, explain that you are seeking help for the problem you identified in your planning session, and set up your first appointment.

Record your observations, taking care to consider the following questions:

- How easy was it to locate the clinic's phone number, and information about your services? Was it easily accessible in the phone book and online?

- When you called, did you get an automated greeting, a voicemail machine or a live person? If you were asked to leave a voicemail, did the outgoing message let you know what information you should include, and when you would be getting a call back?

- Did the phone number you located in the phone book or online connect you directly with the staffer who can set up the appointment, or were you transferred to someone else?

- If a live person picked up, were you put on hold? If so, for how long?

- Did the receptionist/scheduler explain to you clearly what you should expect at your first appointment? Did he give you enough information? Too much information?

- Were you able to schedule your assessment during this first phone call?

- Did you have to speak with multiple people to schedule the appointment?

- Did the receptionist/scheduler:
    - Offer directions to the appointment?
    - Offer alternate ways of getting to the center?
    - Offer appointment times that wouldn't interfere with a work or childcare schedule?

49

- ▸ Explain what you should bring with you to the appointment with regard to insurance or other paperwork?

  - ▸ Ask you if you had any logistical concerns about getting to your first appointment?

  - ▸ Use terminology that could be confusing to the typical customer?

- How soon could you get an appointment?

- Did you end the phone call feeling reassured about what to expect from the first appointment?

- Were you given the opportunity to ask questions or express concerns you might have about scheduling or transportation to your first appointment?

- Did you receive a reminder phone call about your appointment? If so, was it left on your voicemail, or did the receptionist/scheduler keep trying until he got you in person?

Step Two: The Initial Impression

Travel to the facility as a customer would. If you were given directions, be sure to follow them as if you had never driven to the facility before. When you arrive, try to see the facility as if for the first time. Announce yourself to the front desk staff, answer any questions they ask, and fill out all the paperwork.

Record your observations, taking care to consider the following questions:

- If the receptionist gave you directions to the facility over the phone, were the directions accurate and easy to follow?

- Is parking available? Is it difficult to find a place to park? If you have to pay to park, did the receptionist let you know this in advance when you made your appointment?

- Is the facility accessible by public transportation?

- Is the reception area easy to locate and clearly marked?

- How does the physical environment make you feel? Is the reception area warm and inviting or does it feel sterile?

- Is the environment calm, or does it seem chaotic? Try to identify which details make it so.

Step Three: The Intake/Assessment Process

Complete the entire intake process, filling out the required paperwork and submitting to any required exams and tests. Be sure to participate in the process just as a typical client would; if clients are required to undress and/or take a urine test, you should do the same. Are clients required to do something you would refuse to do?

Record your observations, taking care to consider the following questions:

- Did you feel that you had adequate privacy to discuss personal information with the receptionist? At any point were you able to overhear another customer's conversation?

- How much paperwork were you asked to fill out? Is the paperwork clear? Were you asked for any information that you didn't know the answer to that you should have been told to bring with you?

- Does the family member accompany the client throughout the intake process? Were you asked at any point if you'd prefer that your family member not accompany you?

- How long did you have to wait in the waiting room?

- How many staff members did you deal with? Was there a single person guiding you through the process, or did you feel that you were being passed off from one staffer to another?

- Did you feel rushed at any time?

- Was the treatment process clearly explained to you? Were you told what to expect from your next visit?

- Were you introduced to counselors and/or staff members that you'll be working with in the future?

(51)

Step Four: Transfer Between Levels of Care

Go through the process of being transferred between levels of care. Record your observations and consider the following questions:

- How much paperwork is involved in the transfer? Is there redundancy in the paperwork? Are you being asked the same questions that you answered during the intake process?

- Does the transition feel smooth?

- Have you been given information to prepare you for what to expect in the next stage?

- Do you feel you are being adequately guided through the process?

- Do you understand what is expected of you?

This is not an exhaustive list of questions. It's only a few suggestions based on issues that other organizations have identified during their walk-through process. The biggest question is, "What is the experience like for you? Would you want to purchase this service?"

Final Considerations

After you've completed the walk-through, taking copious notes throughout, record your overall impressions, and consider these two questions:

1) What surprised you most during your walk-through?

2) What two things would you most want to change?

STUDY and ACT on the Results

Now that you've completed the walk-through and recorded your experience, you are ready to use the knowledge gained from the walk-through to take the first steps in making positive changes in your organization. After completing the walk-through, you and other staff members who participated should have detailed notes about your own impressions, and staff perspectives. As part of your wrap-up, you should:

- Use your notes to make a list of areas and practices that need improvement, as well as a list of things that worked well

- Meet with the change team to discuss what worked well in the walk-through, and what needs improvement

- If you were given a specific aim prior to the walk-through, sort the ideas and observations related directly to your project from those that are unrelated

- Discuss the ideas generated by the walk-through with your executive sponsor. If you were given a specific aim to address prior to the walk-through, you should discuss problems that seem to relate to that aim. However, you should inform her about potential problems you observed that weren't directly related to your aim so that the executive sponsor may choose to address them in another project.

When a Walk-through May Not Be the Best Tool

The walk-through is one of the most useful ways to identify problems in a service system that inhibit client access to and retention in treatment. However, there are some cases where the walk-through may not be the most useful way to uncover which areas of services are problematic.

During the walk-through, management or staff put themselves in the customer's shoes to better understand customer needs and identify which aspects of the system can be changed to improve the way care is delivered. Therefore, the walk-through is most useful when the main flaws in an organization's system are related to customer care and perception—the "front end" of the business, or the direct clinical services.

The walk-through described in this section may be less useful in instances where the underlying problems lie behind the scenes, in the administrative processes that the customer is not privy to. For example, long waiting periods may be the result of an inefficient computer system. Though the client certainly is negatively affected by this inefficiency, the executive sponsor or change leader would not likely be able to identify this flaw when conducting the walk-through in the "customer" role. In other words, though it's clear that a problem exists, it's difficult to learn from the walk-through where the original flaw lies. In such instances, staff input can be crucial to identifying the problem and implementing a solution.

"I have been pleased to see a number of organizations benefit from understanding that they are not alone in their strategic planning efforts. The same challenges of a fast-moving marketplace that make strategic planning more important than ever, also leave providers with little time to plan. BHB is a great tool for learning, sharing, and readying your organization for the future. " — Mat Roosa, ACSW, LCSW-R, BHB Coach

Find your balance and master the opportunities in front of you!

When you enroll in *BHbusiness: Mastering Essential Business Operations*, you'll be grouped with a learning network of peer organizations as you take one course at a time. You will participate in a range of educational activities, including:

- *Online courses taught by expert faculty*
- *Small group/individual consultation*
- *Coaching*
- *Team projects*

Faculty includes:

- Mike Lardiere, Vice President HIT & Strategic Development, National Council for Behavioral Health
- Kim Johnson, Deputy Director, NIATx, University of Wisconsin-Madison

The BHbusiness initiative is funded by the Substance Abuse and Mental Health Services Administration under Contract number: HHSS283201200001C, Ref: 283-12-0392.

Substance Abuse and Mental Health Services Administration
www.samhsa.gov • 1-877-SAMHSA-7 (1-877-726-4727)

SAAS
STATE ASSOCIATIONS OF
ADDICTION SERVICES

MENTAL HEALTH FIRST AID
NATIONAL COUNCIL
FOR BEHAVIORAL HEALTH
Healthy Minds. Strong Communities.

NIATx™

AHP
Advocates for
Human Potential, Inc.

A Case Study: The Walk-through

About the Organization

St. Christopher's Inn in Garrison, New York, is the oldest freestanding shelter in the state of New York, having celebrated its centennial in 2009. Through its shelter, St. Christopher's offers housing and meals to homeless men, the majority of whom struggle with addiction. The agency operates a licensed outpatient treatment program for men at the shelter and for people in the community. The homeless shelter is funded solely through benefactors and fund-raising.

St. Christopher's hoped to address two key issues with a NIATx change project. For the first time in its history, St. Christopher's Inn had a waiting list for the shelter. This signified a change in use patterns, and indicated to agency administration that shelter capacity could be expanded. Second, St. Christopher's wanted to increase the percentage of shelter residents who also participated in addiction treatment. When the project began, 53 percent of men living at the shelter attended addiction treatment groups. Agency administrators knew that increasing this figure would benefit the individuals involved and increase revenue through Medicaid and private payment for addiction treatment.

The walk-through

During a walk-through, a staff member posed as a person seeking admission to the shelter and addiction treatment. The walk-through uncovered the following issues:

53

- It took the admissions department an average of 2.5 hours to return calls because of the limited number of phone lines and staff break schedules that left the phone unattended over the lunch hour.
- Caller frustration at being routed to voicemail or being placed on a waiting list for the shelter.
- Duplication of paperwork in the intake and admission process.
- Delays at admission because of the limited number of staff trained to admit new clients.

Information gathered during the walk-through helped the change team select the aims for their change project.

Aims

- Decrease waiting time
- Increase admissions

Changes

The change team added a phone line in the admissions department to accommodate more callers. They also adjusted admissions staff schedules so that the phone was covered throughout the business day including the lunch hour. They trained additional staff to complete admissions and also eliminated the unnecessary admissions paperwork.

Results

These changes made it possible for prospective clients to talk directly to a staff member more quickly. More calls were answered live, and the average wait time for direct phone contact decreased from 2.5 hours to just under 15 minutes. Eliminating unnecessary paperwork and adding more staff trained to complete admissions made the process much smoother.

In Summary

The knowledge that you gain from the walk-through will help you understand where your priorities should be and what kinds of changes will ultimately have the biggest impact on customer perceptions and the budget.

Understanding what your customers want and need— and what's working for them and what isn't in the way you currently do business — is critical if you want to make changes that matter. By "matter," we mean that the changes will improve the quality of care provided to clients and will have a positive impact on the business (by driving up revenues and/or driving down costs).

Chapter 5: Leadership and Teamwork

Although we emphasize that improvement initiatives should focus on processes and not people, the importance of the personnel involved in the change effort—from the executive sponsor to affected staff members—cannot be overstated. A change project is only as good as the quality of its teamwork, the strength of its leadership, and its reception in the organization as a whole.

This is the human side of the change process, where the different skills and strengths of the individuals in your organization can come together to make the project a success. How does the change leader keep the project moving forward? What does each member of the change team bring to the table, and how can the team work together successfully? How will the project be received by staff not directly involved in the project, but who will nonetheless be affected by its outcome?

A change project's success depends on a variety of factors, some of which are within your control, and some of which aren't. One thing you can control is setting up the change team for success. By thoughtfully choosing who will participate in the project, clearly defining roles and responsibilities, facilitating productive teamwork, and engaging and informing all staff in the change process, you create optimal conditions for the project. Under such conditions, experiments can flourish in a controlled environment, and each player is in a position to contribute all that he or she has to offer.

In this section, we discuss the roles and responsibilities of the key players in the change effort and offer tips for how to select people to fill these roles. We also present a tool for effective and systematic group decision-making, and offer strategies for engaging staff in the change effort. In short, we help you create the kind of leadership structure and interpersonal dynamics needed to set your project on the right path to accomplishing its goal.

The Executive Sponsor

The executive sponsor is the instigating force for change within the organization, the person who makes the project happen. The executive sponsor identifies the need for change, articulates the goal, and puts into place the mechanisms required to carry out the change process. While not necessarily directing every move on a micro level (that role rests with the change leader), the executive sponsor oversees the project, monitoring it closely enough to remove obstacles and ensure that progress is being made toward the goal. Additionally, the executive sponsor serves as an advocate and publicist for the project within the organization.

The executive sponsor is responsible for:

1. **Identifying the problem:** By completing a walk-through, using existing data, and interviewing or holding focus groups with staff and clients, the executive sponsor identifies key problems and some potential reasons why they are problems.

2. **Articulating the project's purpose:** Based on the problem identification, what is the project's purpose and how does it fit with the overall goals of the organization? What do you hope to accomplish by the end of the project? (What is the project aim?) For example, an aim might be to eliminate the wait list, or to retain 80 percent of clients through their first month of treatment. The executive sponsor should be able to clearly articulate the goal that the change team is expected to meet, and should communicate it throughout the organization.

3. **Appointing a change leader and change team:** The executive sponsor selects the change leader using the criteria in this chapter. The change leader may help in selecting staff to participate in the change team.

4. **Creating boundaries and guidelines for the project**, including:

   - Developing a budget if there is one, as well as a process for approving additional expenses.

   - Creating explicit guidelines as to what the team may ask of other staff in terms of time or resources.

   - Empowering the change leader by granting her broad authority and clearly communicating the parameters of that authority.

5. **Monitoring the project's progress.** This includes:

   - Meeting regularly with the change leader

   - Reviewing progress with respect to the project's original plan

   - Ensuring that the project remains focused and goal-oriented

   - Attending occasional team meetings

   - Reviewing and responding to minutes from team meetings not attended

   - Reviewing proposed plans and offering feedback

   - Confirming that all decisions being made are based on data

   - Helping the team troubleshoot and overcome barriers

   - Keeping the team focused on processes, not people

   - Limiting the entire project to six months or less—consisting of several PDSA Cycles conducted in rapid succession for much shorter periods of time

6. **Advocating for the project:** The executive sponsor serves as an ambassador for the project to the rest of the organization, meaning that she is responsible for:

   - Allocating time and resources to the project, making sure the change leader gets whatever resources (including time) he needs to manage the project

   - Publicizing the project throughout the organization, both at its outset and as it progresses

- Engaging staff in the project
- Keeping the board, other senior leadership, and external stakeholders interested and invested in the project
- Working to avoid conflicts between the project and other members of the organization, and resolving any conflicts that do arise

7. Offering positive reinforcement: The executive sponsor should offer encouragement to the team and staff, and should offer appreciation for a job well done.

The Change Leader

The change leader, who is selected by the executive sponsor, is responsible for directing the project in its day-to-day activities, such as running meetings and pilot tests, and for serving as the link between the change team and the executive sponsor.

Specifically, the change leader is responsible for:

1. Project Management

- Serving as liaison between the executive sponsor and the change team, communicating progress reports to the executive sponsor, and sharing feedback with the team
- Creating an outline and schedule for the project, including deadlines
- Monitoring those deadlines and making sure they are met
- Developing, installing, and supervising a simple system for collecting and reviewing data
- Delegating tasks to members of the change team, taking care to match each team member with a task that suits his or her skill set
- Following up on assignments to make sure that the assigned task has been completed in a timely and thorough manner
- Directing pilot tests and helping the team overcome obstacles that arise

2. Running Change Team Meetings

- Arranging meeting times and locations
- Creating an agenda for each meeting
- Keeping the team on topic and avoiding unproductive sidetracks
- Actively fostering an atmosphere of inclusivity and full participation
- Recording key decisions
- Facilitating group discussion and decision making

The change team should meet frequently. Some groups have "stand up" meetings where they check in for 10 minutes every week and have a longer meeting only at the end of each change cycle. Other groups meet weekly or biweekly for an hour. Only meet for the time required for following up on tasks and ensuring continued energy and enthusiasm. Also, meet when a change cycle is complete to review the data and determine next steps.

3. Maintaining Energy

- Keeping the team motivated and engaged in the project
- Offering positive reinforcement and encouragement

Appointing a Change leader

The executive sponsor 's duties include appointing a change leader and assembling a change team. The change leader has numerous and challenging responsibilities that demand an impressive set of skills and characteristics. The executive sponsor should thus take great care in deciding who will lead the change team. Here are some factors to consider while making a selection:

1. Logistical Considerations

- **Time:** The change leader should be given enough time to manage the project. Two hours per week seems to be a typical amount of time for the change leader to devote to a change project.
- **Position in hierarchy:** The change leader should be someone who reports to the executive sponsor in her official job, or should be given the right to report to the executive sponsor regarding the change project without going through multiple levels of hierarchy.
- **First-hand knowledge:** The change leader should be someone who's involved in some way with the process under scrutiny, but not married to the current process.

2. Authority Within the Organization

- **Peer credibility:** It's essential that the change leader be someone who is liked and re-spected by other members of the organization, and he should have influence with his peers. If the change leader lacks legitimacy in the eyes of the change team members or staff involved in the change project, the project will likely not succeed.
- **Authority:** The change leader needs to be comfortable interacting with key players at all levels of the organization; she should be someone who would not hesitate to call the CEO at home at night to discuss the project.

3. Skills and Personal Characteristics

- **Organized:** Running the logistics of the effort means juggling many balls at once, which will require good organizational skills.

- **Independent:** The change leader should be someone comfortable in the role of leader—someone who's bold, takes initiative, and doesn't wait to be told what to do.

- **Good at delegating:** The change leader will necessarily be required to delegate certain tasks to team members. Not only does this require a high level of organization, but it also requires the change leader to be someone good at recognizing the strengths and weaknesses in others.

- **Persistent:** The project may meet with a few setbacks before it sees success; it's important that the change leader take these setbacks in stride and keep at it.

- **Innovative and curious:** Look for someone who's naturally inclined to challenge the status quo and think outside the box for creative solutions.

- **Comfortable with data:** The change leader needs to both recognize the importance of data and be comfortable with collecting and analyzing it. If this is a deficit in an otherwise strong change candidate, add a data manager to the change team who can work with the change leader on this critical aspect of the project.

- **Focused:** A scattered change leader will result in a scattered change project; make sure that the leader is someone capable of focusing on one thing at a time, and does not get easily distracted or driven off course.

- **Optimistic:** An optimistic disposition is essential; someone who is easily discouraged or quick to see the downside of things will be unlikely to sustain the necessary atmosphere and energy.

Assembling the Change Team

The executive sponsor assembles the change team. It may be helpful to ask the change leader for his input in selecting team members, as he will bring a different perspective and may be more familiar with the potential team members from interacting with them in his day-to-day position.

One of the greatest benefits of working in a team is that each member brings his or her own experiences, knowledge, and skills to the table. Ideally, this variety of personalities functions together fluidly, and the brainstorming and decision-making processes benefit from the breadth of skills and ideas present at the table.

In a well-balanced team, the weaknesses of one member will be compensated for by the strengths of another, and vice versa, so the goal is to assemble a team that collectively possesses all the skills required to make the project a success. Once you've decided who you'd like to include on the team, send each one a formal, written invitation that explains what the project is about and what responsibilities will come with the job. Be sure to clearly communicate that this is a temporary addition to his or her regular responsibilities. If you are able to remove something from his plate, articulate what that temporary change of responsibilities is.

Here are some tips for assembling a team that has all the right components:

- Choose people who work in different areas of the system being studied. For example, if you're scrutinizing the admissions process, include a staffer who books appointments as well as someone who performs assessments.

- Include different categories of employees, such as counselors and back-office staff, to get a wide range of perspectives.

- Include staff who work in the area where the change(s) will be implemented as well as other staff who will be affected by the change(s).

- Choose people with a wide and diverse range of strengths, as the team will benefit greatly from the skills and ideas of different types of people. For example, choosing team members who are detail oriented, and logical thinkers, as well as team members who are more artistically or creatively minded, will produce a well-rounded and balanced team.

- Include staff who don't work in the area under scrutiny to get an outside perspective.

- Include a client or former client on the team to get a customer's perspective.

The **Change Project Form** on the pages that follow provides a way for you to document your team roles and your change project progress.

Team Decision Making: Nominal Group Technique

Teamwork isn't always easy, particularly when a group of creative, highly opinionated minds get together. Different personalities may produce conflicting ideas; this is a good thing—it's a sign that you've assembled a team with a diverse range of abilities and perspectives. It can be difficult, however, to reconcile all these ideas and decide which one to run with. The Nominal Group Technique is a helpful tool to solve this problem[1].

The Nominal Group Technique (NGT) is a team-based decision-making process that may be used to either identify problems in a process, or brainstorm and prioritize potential solutions to test. An NGT session starts off with a question, posed by the change leader (or executive sponsor) to the team that's meant to explain to the participants what the objective of the meeting is. From there, all members of the team individually brainstorm, and then come together as a group to share their ideas. Then the ideas are all discussed, and the team votes to determine which idea to run with.

Change Project Form

PROJECT CHARTER for (name of organization)	
1. CHANGE PROJECT TITLE	
2. AIM STATEMENT: What are you trying to accomplish? Use this template.	Reduce/Increase (choose one) _____ by (%) _____ from (baseline) _____ to (goal) _____ by (end date) ___/___/___. Example: Reduce no-shows to assessment appointments by 50% from an average no-show rate of 80% to 40% by February 1, 2012.
3. Specific LOCATION, SERVICE, PROGRAM or LEVEL OF CARE	
4. PROJECT START DATE and END DATE	Start ▓ ▓ End ▓ ▓
5. Who is your CUSTOMER for this project?	▓
6. EXECUTIVE SPONSOR	▓
7. CHANGE LEADER	▓
8. DATA COORDINATOR	▓
9. CHANGE TEAM MEMBERS/ROLE on the team	▓
10. What DATA will be collected and how will you collect data to MEASURE the impact of change?	What data? ▓ How will you collect it? ▓
11. What is the expected IMPACT of this change project on the organization's FINANCES, CUSTOMERS, STAFF?	▓

Visit the NIATx.net Resource Center "Forms and Templates" section to download this form.

Change Project Form

RAPID-CYCLE TESTING

62

Rapid Cycle #

Cycle Begin Date:	Cycle End Date:

What is the idea/change to be tested?

P	**PLAN:** *What steps are you specifically making to test this idea/change? Who is responsible? How it will get done?*
D	**DO:** *What steps did you implement? Document any problems and unexpected observations from the PLAN.*
S	**STUDY:** *What were the results? How do they compare with baseline measure?*
A	**ACT:** *What is your next step? Adopt? Adapt? Abandon?*

Rapid Cycle #

Cycle Begin Date:	Cycle End Date:

What is the idea/change to be tested?

P	**PLAN:** *What steps are you specifically making to test this idea/change? Who is responsible? How it will get done?*
D	**DO:** *What steps did you implement? Document any problems and unexpected observations from the PLAN.*
S	**STUDY:** *What were the results? How do they compare with baseline measure?*
A	**ACT:** *What is your next step? Adopt? Adapt? Abandon?*

Note: Continue to conduct PDSA Cycles until you know the change is an improvement for your overall aim.

Visit the NIATx.net Resource Center "Forms and Templates" section to download this form.

Change Project Form

EVALUATION AND SUSTAIN PLAN

Project Outcomes (only complete once the project is finished)

1. What was the project **END DATE** (when you stopped making changes)?	
2. What did you **LEARN** (e.g., what were some unexpected outcomes or lessons learned from your change efforts)?	
3. What was the **FINANCIAL IMPACT** of this change project? (e.g. Increased revenue? Reduced costs? Increased staff retention?)	

Sustainability Plan (only complete if you are sustaining the changes)

A. Who is the **SUSTAIN LEADER**?	
B. What CHANGES do you want **TO SUSTAIN**?	
C. What **SUSTAIN STEPS** are being taken to ensure that the changes stay in place and that it is not possible to revert back to the old way of doing things?	
D. What is the **TARGET SUSTAIN MEASURE**, i.e. the point at which the Change Team would intervene to get the project back on track?	
E. What system is in place to effectively **MONITOR the SUSTAIN MEASURE**?	
Additional Notes:	

63

Visit the NIATx.net Resource Center "Forms and Templates" section to download this form.

Nominal Group Technique is not only a systematic way to avoid the chaos that often comes with brainstorming; it also ensures full participation and equality among the members of the group. Everyone shares their ideas, and all the ideas are given equal weight, helping to avoid a scenario in which the more forceful or extroverted personalities in the room dominate the decision-making process.

What follows is a step-by-step guide, aimed at the change leader, to help navigate the NGT process.

> Nominal Group Technique is best used with groups of 5–9 people; fewer than 5 and there will not be adequate participation, and more than 9 can make for an overly long and chaotic process. If you would like to conduct an NGT session with more than 9 people, split the participants evenly into subgroups, and have each subgroup complete Steps 1 through 4 (silent idea generation through voting) individually. Then, schedule a lunch break and use that time to record the top 5 ideas from each subgroup, creating a master list. After lunch, bring all the subgroups together and proceed with the session as a single group.

Stage One: Pre-Meeting Preparation

In the lead-up to the meeting, the change leader should prepare by:

- **Developing the question that she will pose to the group:** As stated above, the question should illustrate the objective of the meeting, whether it's to identify problems or prioritize solutions. The question should give participants a sense of the desired depth and breadth of their responses. For example:

"We have identified that our wait list for treatment is due to our long intake process. What are all the changes we could make to shorten the intake process? When we discharge patients from the hospital, they don't fill their prescriptions so they are being readmitted really quickly. What are all the things you can think of that we could try to make sure our patients get their medications?"

Identify the problem to be addressed. If you know the cause of the problem, identify the cause, and then ask the members of the team for ideas about how to solve the problem. If you don't know the cause of the problem, you may want to add an extra step in which the group identifies the potential causes, uses the NGT to select a cause, and then goes through the NGT again to identify solutions that address the chosen possible cause.

- **Getting the logistics in order.** The change leader will need to prepare the logistics of the meeting by reserving a room large enough to hold all the participants, with tables that allow the participants to face each other and easily engage. The change leader should also bring the necessary supplies, which include:
    - Print-outs of the question being posed (enough for each participant to get one)

- ▸ Flip charts
- ▸ Enough pens and paper for each participant
- ▸ Index cards or Post-it Notes
- ▸ Masking tape

- **Preparing an opening statement.** The statement should welcome the group to the meeting and clarify its purpose, explain how the process will work, and how the results will be used.

Stage Two: Lead the Meeting

Deliver your opening statement and pose your prepared question to the group (hand out the printed copies, as well). Then begin the session by leading the group through the following steps:

Step 1: Silent idea generation

After presenting the question, give the participants up to 15 minutes to meditate in silence on the question and write down their ideas. Ideas can be jotted down quickly, and there is no need for complete sentences. This step serves to give the participants quiet time to think about the question before jumping in, and it fosters an atmosphere of collective effort, without encouraging competition. When the participants finish writing, give them a few extra minutes to see if they come up with additional ideas. Sometimes the ideas written at the last minute out of discomfort with doing nothing actually lead to the best change projects.

(65)

Step 2: Round robin recording of ideas

Once each participant has jotted down all her ideas, the next step is to share them with the group. During the round robin, the change leader goes around the table, asking each participant to present one of his or her ideas that hasn't already been posted by someone else. The change leader writes each idea on the board, and numbers them in the order presented. Once the leader has gone around the whole table and has recorded an idea from each participant, the cycle repeats itself until every idea has been recorded (if a participant has run out of ideas while the round robin is still going, he may choose to "pass").

> The change leader may ask questions for clarification, but she should record it using the same phrasing used by the participant expressing the idea, rather than paraphrasing.

The round robin step of NGT is an important one because it ensures that everyone's ideas will be heard and given equal weight. The structure of the round robin can also generate additional ideas, as a participant may have an idea sparked by listening to someone else's idea. Furthermore, by putting each idea up on the board without labeling it with a name, the round robin serves to disassociate the person from the idea, so that participants don't take things personally. And finally, the round robin is a clear, systematic way of sorting through a large number of ideas.

Step 3: Serial discussion of ideas

After the ideas have all been written on the board, the group discusses them one by one. This step allows for clarification of an idea and it allows the group members to work through disagreements. Every idea should be given a discussion to make sure that no idea gets lost. It also helps identify duplication that may have been missed in the round robin process.

Step 4: Preliminary voting

After discussion, the group votes to determine which idea to run with.

Each participant is given a certain number of "points." The number of points is arbitrary, but the number must be the same for all participants; we tend to use between 3 and 5 points, as it's small enough to force choice but large enough to allow participants to weight their response. The participant then distributes these points or votes to the ideas as he sees fit, giving more points to the ideas he prefers and less (or none) to the ones he doesn't. If desired, he can give all his points to a single idea, or some points to every idea.

Participants may vote with stickers, using pen and pencil to make stars on their selections from the posted ideas or by writing the selected ideas on a secret ballot. If the leader is participating in the voting process, she should go last so as to not influence the other team members' choices.

If there is a clear winner, then you may move on setting up the change project. If there is a tie or a close vote, then there is one more step in the process.

Step 5: Discuss the Preliminary Vote

This is an opportunity to discuss ideas that received inconsistent voting patterns, for example, if it seems as though a particular idea got too many or too few votes. If there's a tie, it's an opportunity to discuss the merits of each idea as the first one to try. Sometimes it becomes clear through discussion that one project would require a substantial amount of pre-work, while the other could be implemented quickly and easily. Sometimes with discussion it's determined that one change project is really a precursor step in another project and that it would be best to address the steps in the process in the order that they happen. The discussion of why people chose particular options and how they might be implemented can lead to more clarity of purpose and a better change project overall.

Step 6: Final Vote

Now, the group votes again, using the same system as before, to determine the final decision.

Engaging Staff in the Change Process

As the executive sponsor, one of your responsibilities is to serve as the advocate for the change project throughout the organization. One critical aspect to this role is engaging all the staff in the organization, from receptionists to clinicians, in the project at hand and in the larger goal of creating a culture of continuous improvement.

Why are staff attitudes so important? Even staff who are not on the change team are an important part of the testing process and are even more crucial when a change is being implemented and sustained. If a project runs up against indifference or, worse, resistance from staff, it will make every step of the process more difficult and can significantly impede or derail progress.

When a change project is able to push forward despite staff resistance, negative attitudes can continue to cause problems and decrease the likelihood that the changes will be sustained. (This is why staff attitudes are used as a predictor in the Sustainability Model in chapter 11.) Although the immediate goal of a change project is to address a specific aim, each project should also move the organization closer to that ideal culture of improvement. Pushing a project through an uncooperative staff environment is not conducive to creating this type of culture, and it's likely that you'll keep encountering resistance in subsequent projects.

It's important to remember that an engaged, enthusiastic staff has a great deal to offer a project in terms of ideas, insights, and personal experience. Each staff person has a unique point of view and sees the organization's services through a different lens, informed by his or her role in the organization. While the organization's leadership might know how things work in theory and how a particular process is meant to run, employees who are a part of these processes on a practical, day-to-day basis know how they actually work, where problems arise, what clients do and don't like, and which processes aren't running as efficiently as possible. Their insights and ideas for improvement can be valuable, and you certainly don't want to miss out on hearing them because staff members are unenthusiastic or don't feel like they are an important part of the project.

Furthermore, resistant staff may be right: They may resist change because it's a bad idea. Making sure there is buy-in ensures that everyone is heading in the same direction and prevents errors in leadership's judgment from implementing bad policy and procedures.

In short, although it's possible for an uncooperative staff to derail a project, don't look at them as an obstacle, but rather an asset. Your goal is not their indifferent cooperation, but their enthusiastic participation in not only the project at hand but in creating an organization-wide culture of improvement.

To understand how to go about engaging staff in the project, it's essential to first put yourself in their shoes to understand why they might be indifferent or resistant to the project in the first place. Consider the following reasons people might be wary of an improvement project:

- **Skepticism:** They don't believe that the change project will yield improvements, or that a change can be successfully implemented and sustained.

- **Lack of understanding:** They don't understand why a change is necessary, and how it will help the organization.

- **Defensiveness:** They are concerned that the project's purpose is to assign blame for poor performance, or that the project itself implies that staff aren't performing adequately.

- **Anxiety:** They are unsure about what's going to happen and how it will affect their responsibilities and workload, or they feel that the project is being forced on them and that they have no input into what happens.

Overcoming these reasons for resistance to the project essentially comes down to two key strategies: communicating with staff and involving them in the project. The problems mentioned above stem mostly from feelings of powerlessness and of a lack knowledge about the project's purpose, of how process improvement generally works, and of the progress being made on the particular project.

By communicating with staff about the project and opening up channels for them to get involved and offer their own opinions and insights, you can get them on board with the project and reap the benefits of their participation.

Communication

Being well informed about the project is reassuring for staff, and can convince skeptics that change can be beneficial to them as well as the clients and the organization. There are many ways to keep staff informed about the project, such as all-staff meetings, e-mail bulletins, newsletters, or posting notices in the break room. Choose whichever makes the most sense for your circumstances, and make sure the information is accessible to everyone. The last thing you want to do is inadvertently exclude certain employees. However you choose to communicate, the key point to keep in mind is that communication should be regular and continuous; information should be shared with the staff not only at the beginning of the project, but throughout the project and at completion.

At the beginning of the project, take care to communicate:

- The purpose of the project: Why change is necessary and how it will improve the organization.

- How process improvement works, and specifically how the project at hand will work. Explain how long it will last, how testing works, and what may be asked of them during the testing process.

- The basics of PDSA Cycles: It's important to let the staff know that PDSA Cycles are by nature short experiments, lasting no longer than a couple weeks (and ideally less than that). If the staff finds a particular test to be overly burdensome, they'll be less resentful if they know that it'll be of short duration.

- How data will be collected, and how the data will be used: Emphasize that the data collection process will be simple and that the results will be shared.

- That the project is focused on processes, not people: Reassure employees that no one is being blamed for anything, that no fingers are being pointed, and that the problems lie with the processes, not the people executing them.

- That you welcome their ideas and feedback, and that you are taking their positions into account as you move forward with the project.

Throughout the project:

- Regularly communicate updates as well as any progress or accomplishments.

- Share data from pilot testing: Post it in the break room or send out a staff-wide e-mail. Remember to present the data visually (see Chapter 7) so that staff can fully appreciate the impact of positive changes.

- Express appreciation: Thank the change team members and other staff for their hard work and let them know that you value their contributions.

Share any positive customer feedback so that staff know that the changes really are helping the clients.

Involving Staff

Communication goes both ways: In addition to informing staff about the project, you'll want to involve them by soliciting their ideas and feedback. Empower them by making them a part of the process. Some key points:

- **Use the walk-through:** When you perform the walk-through, remember to ask the employees you encounter for their ideas for improvement or thoughts about what works well and what doesn't. These are the people who deal with this process every day, so they'll surely have useful opinions.

- **Create a system for offering feedback:** How should staff communicate their ideas or feedback about the project? Who should they communicate those ideas to? Staff may be more hesitant to get involved if they don't know the appropriate way to do so. If there is a system set up for this purpose, employees may feel more inclined to participate.

A few more points to keep in mind...

- Be on their side: When your staff members know that you are taking their concerns into account, they'll be less anxious about what's going to happen.

- Think about changes that will help the staff, such as reducing paperwork, assigning more staff during busier shifts, or making the facilities more inviting.

The case study that follows describes an improvement initiative at CAB Health and Recovery Services, Inc. in Massachusetts. It provides an excellent example of how to engage staff in a change project, and the impressive achievements that may result.

A Case Study: Engaging Staff

About the organization

CAB Health and Recovery Services in Massachusetts, now known as Northeast Behavioral Health, is a private, nonprofit human service agency that provides mental health, substance abuse, and community education and prevention services to residents in Boston and surrounding areas. Services include outpatient mental health clinics, inpatient and outpatient substance abuse treatment and prevention, and community education and prevention initiatives.

Aims

• Increase admissions

• Increase continuation

Changes

CAB's outpatient substance abuse services were operating below capacity, which was affecting its ability to provide needed services to clients—and staff morale. CAB assigned a project leader to work with the agency's director of ambulatory services to make improvements. Working with clients and staff, they identified problems in the existing system and worked on solutions to increase client access to outpatient services—and generate revenue. Throughout the project, the project leaders made a conscious effort to involve staff, to take their opinions and concerns into account, and to build enthusiasm for change. Their strategies included:

• Conducting a staff survey at the beginning of the change project. In the survey results, staff identified communication with management as a problem. To address this, the project leaders scheduled one-on-one interviews with staff to get their input on ways to solve problems such as inefficiencies, duplicate paperwork, and the lack of dedicated private space for counseling sessions.

• The project leaders instituted weekly all-staff meetings for teambuilding.

• The leaders shared important data, which helped get reluctant staff on board. For example, data highlighting problems with revenue helped convince wary staff that changes to the scheduling and billing systems were necessary.

• Project leaders identified five main problem areas with the outpatient services. Then, they broke each one into smaller components to help staff see the exact source for a specific problem.

• Project leaders consulted with staff to both pinpoint problems, create solutions, and refine changes during pilot tests.

- The team implemented changes that benefitted, staff and clients (creating a more welcoming environment) and had a positive impact on revenue (eliminating efficiencies).

- Project leaders considered staff workload when redesigning systems to accommodate increased volume, re-working existing staff roles to meet the new needs, and taking staff well-being into account.

Results

CAB's effort to involve staff resulted in a successful project and a more satisfied staff. The effort was not entirely smooth: CAB experienced a 25 percent staff turnover in the first six months of the project. Since then the turnover rate has dropped to three percent, staff morale has improved, and clients, staff, and the bottom line have all benefited.

In Summary

The NIATx model of process improvement insists that organizations define their improvement aims up front. The executive sponsor plays a key role in defining a change team's aim and authorizing the time and resources required to complete a successful change project. The executive sponsor selects a change leader, ideally someone who has the ability to influence all levels of the organization. Together the executive sponsor and the change leader assemble a change team that works to improve a process that affects the targeted aim.

72

Chapter 6: Rapid-Cycle Testing

The fifth principle of the NIATx model is what we call rapid-cycle testing. Structured around what's known as the PDSA (Plan-Do-Study-Act) Cycle, rapid-cycle testing is used to quickly evaluate the impact of potential changes on a given aim[1]. In rapid-cycle testing, the executive sponsor, change leader, or team comes up with ideas for changes to test, and then tests each of those changes in quick succession for a short time on a limited test pool. During each test (a.k.a. PDSA Cycle), the team collects and analyzes data relevant to its chosen aim to determine whether the change has produced a desirable effect on performance levels. Depending on the outcome of that analysis, the team may decide to abandon the change completely and begin testing an entirely new change; adapt the change for further improvement and retest the modified version; or adopt the change, testing it again on a slightly larger scale, or in conjunction with other changes that have already proven successful in testing. In any case, the team uses the knowledge it has gained from one testing cycle to improve subsequent cycles. A new procedure is only implemented on a full scale once it has been proven in testing to yield significant improvement in regard to the project's aim.

Process Improvement

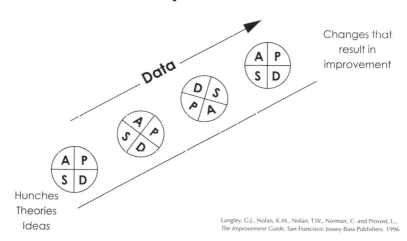

Langley, G.J., Nolan, K.M., Nolan, T.W., Norman, C. and Provost, L., *The Improvement Guide*, San Francisco: Jossey-Bass Publishers. 1996

In rapid-cycle testing, a series of short PDSA Cycles are performed in quick succession, for a short period of time[1].

The rapid-cycle testing stage of a change project starts with three questions:

1. What are we trying to accomplish?

2. How will we know the change is an improvement?

3. What changes can we test that will result in an improvement?

Through the course of rapid-cycle testing, what starts off as a hunch ("I suspect we can decrease the number of no-shows by offering transportation to our clinic from downtown") evolves into a clearly defined, evidence-based practice with proven results ("By running a twice-daily shuttle bus to our clinic from downtown, we reduce the number of no-shows from 42 percent to 21 percent"). Furthermore, by experimenting with rapid-cycle testing, you'll ensure that a change yields the kind of improvement you're looking for before you spend the time, energy, and money required to implement it on a full scale.

> The key to rapid-cycle testing is in the name itself: rapid. Each testing cycle, including planning, execution, and analysis, should take no longer than a few weeks. Another key to this method is repetition; in the majority of cases, the team will have to test several changes in quick succession (with each test lasting no longer than a couple days, preferably) to figure out which changes will yield the most improvement, and to refine those changes to maximize benefits. Because each cycle is so short, you'll be able to do more of them, getting better and better with each one, and progressing closer to your goal.

> When to start rapid-cycle testing: This stage comes after the change leader and team have been selected, after the executive sponsor has decided which aim she would like the team to address, and after the team has met and selected a change project via the nominal group process.

The Purpose of Rapid-Cycle Testing, and Why "Rapid" Is Key

When doing rapid-cycle testing, it's critical that you limit the time you spend planning, executing, and analyzing a given change, for a number of reasons:

- **Deadlines:** Setting specific, concrete deadlines forces the team to act and to get things done. By allotting only a couple days for the entire test process, including planning, you avoid the trap of getting so hung up in the planning stage that you never end up making the change. Without a solid timeframe and deadlines, it's easy to let a project drag on and on, particularly when the planning phase of a project seems to be easier than the "doing" phase.

- **Risk reduction:** Short tests minimize the chances of spending lots of time, energy, and money on testing a change that turns out to be ineffective. By testing changes rapidly, you are able to quickly ascertain whether you are headed in the right direction or whether you should choose a new direction entirely. And the stakes are lower: If one direction turns out to be fruitless, that's all right, and you can move on knowing that you haven't wasted much time. Tests that last longer than a month tend to become the new way of doing things even if they have proven unsuccessful.

- **Experimentation:** Short testing cycles allow the team to be more experimental with the changes they decide to test, which often produce surprising results. When you're only committing a couple weeks to a change, you are more willing to think outside the box and test some of the more off-the-wall ideas you've come up with. On the other hand, if the test period was to last for two months, you might be less inclined to take risks because the stakes would be higher.

- **Staff support:** Short tests are less overwhelming for staff, and will produce less resistance and skepticism. Staff are more likely to have an open mind about trying out a new procedure with the knowledge that it is short term. Furthermore, once you decide to institutionalize a change on a full scale, staff may be more enthusiastic because they have seen for themselves how well it worked during testing.

- **Knowledge:** You'll learn from the tests, even if they are not successful, and you can put that knowledge to use in subsequent tests. Shorter tests mean more tests, and more tests means evolution of ideas and refinement of methods. You'll also become better at conducting the tests in the future.

- **Less disruption:** Everyone has had the experience at least once of a large-scale organizational change being implemented without adequate testing (new information systems are the quintessential example). A lot of money, time, and energy has been spent on planning and implementing, but not on testing; staff are dragged away from their normal duties to assist in implementation; efficiency is reduced during the implementation, so the organization and clients all suffer. If staff and clients had been more engaged in planning and testing, the process might not have had to be so large and disruptive. A small change, tested in a small area, or even with one staff person and with a few clients, can identify changes that work well before they are expanded to the whole organization, disrupting only one or a few people's work until a change is proven to work.

A Guide to Conducting Rapid-Cycle Tests

What follows are some key points to help you get started with rapid-cycle testing.

Collect Baseline Data

At this point, you've already answered the first question, "What are we trying to accomplish?" by selecting an aim. Now you need to figure out how you'll know if the changes you're about to test yield improvements with regard to that aim.

You do this by identifying a measure. What data do you already collect that can be used to see if a change is an improvement or not? If you have to collect new data, make it simple. For example, if the aim you've chosen is reducing the amount of time between first contact and first appointment, the important data that you'll want to pay attention to is the average number of days a client must wait from his first contact with the agency to his first appointment. To calculate this, you would document every person who contacts the agency seeking services; recording the date of contact and the day he was first seen. Then you could count the number of days between those two contact points and compute an average for all clients in the week or two or three that you are collecting your data.

Once you've identified the data elements that you need, it's time to collect baseline data. Baseline data refer to the level of performance with regard to your chosen aim before changes are tested or instituted. This is your starting point, the numbers that you are trying to improve. If you don't already collect the information you need to measure whether your change project worked, you'll need to collect this information before you begin testing changes to determine whether those changes are having a positive effect (in this case, decreasing the number of days between first contact and assessment) compared to your baseline data.

Spend two or three weeks collecting baseline data before you start a rapid-cycle test. Make the process uniform by creating a data collection form, deciding how often to collect data, and clearly spelling out how to collect the data. Later, when you are collecting data during your tests, use the same forms and rules to ensure that the two sets of data are truly comparable.

Of course, if you already have the necessary data, then you only need to look at what you have, analyzing the data from a time frame that's comparable to the time you'll be testing your change.

NIATx has created a variety of forms that can be used for collecting and tracking data. See Chapter 7 for examples: **Tracking Starting Clients and Tracking Reschedule Rate for No-shows**. You can also download these forms and others from the Forms and Templates page of the NIATx website at www.niatx.net

Develop Changes to Test

The team should brainstorm to create a list of changes to test that seem promising. Here are some tips for deciding on changes to test:

- Review Promising Practices in Chapter 8, (or visit www.niatx.net for a complete list of Promising Practices) and consider their benefits in regard to the aim you've selected. These practices have been proven effective in NIATx agencies, and there's a good chance they'll work for you. You can also use our Promising Practices as a jumping off point to stir up your own ideas for improvements.
- Use the Nominal Group Technique (see Chapter 5).
- Communicate with other NIATx agencies, getting advice on practices that have worked for them.
- Study your notes and impressions from the walk-through and consider the factors that you thought could be improved or handled better.

Start Small

Start by testing the changes you've come up with in one location, one level of care, and one specific population. Start with a small number of clients, and clearly define the parameters of the test (i.e., outpatient alcohol-abuse clients at the downtown location). It's entirely possible to conduct the first test of a cycle in a single day, on just a few clients. The point is to get a quick feel for whether the change is promising and how it might be made even better. As you conduct more cycles, refining the change as you go along, you can increase the number of test subjects (though the test should remain quick).

Set a Goal for Improvement
Decide how much improvement you'd like to see with regard to your chosen aim, while being both ambitious and realistic. For example, you may decide that you'd like to increase admissions from 20 to 30 clients per week. If you find, as you conduct testing, that you reach your goal easily, you may want to set the bar even higher. Bear in mind that you may have to make multiple changes to meet your goal.

Do one change at a time
If you make multiple changes at once, you won't know which one worked, so you'll be wasting time and effort doing two things differently instead of one. When you analyze the results of the test period, you want to know for sure that any improvement (or deterioration) from baseline is almost certainly due to the single change you were testing. For example, let's say that you are ready to start rapid-cycle testing changes that you hope will reduce waiting time. You come up with two changes that seem promising: double-booking appointments and allowing walk-ins. During the first test, you decide to institute both these new changes for a couple days. The problem here is that whatever the outcome, positive, negative, or neutral, you won't know which factor is responsible. On the other hand, if you give each of these two changes its own separate test period, you'll know for sure whether each one helps or hinders your cause. You need to do this for each change, even if you are testing a promising practice, because what worked for someone else may not work for your organization.

(77)

Essentially, the key here is patience. Even if you're sure that all of your ideas for change will yield great results, test them individually. Then you can start a new test cycle in which you test the successful changes together and make sure that the improvement sticks. When you keep your change cycles short, you'll get to all your ideas within a brief time.

Using PDSA Cycles to Structure Your Test
Each individual rapid-cycle test takes its structure from what's known in the process improvement field as the PDSA (Plan, Do, Study, Act) cycle. The PDSA Cycle works because of its simple and natural flow. Its beauty lies in the fact that it's a reflection of the natural, instinctual process of gathering information and making careful decisions based on an analysis of that information. The PDSA Cycle sets up clearly delineated stages for each test, which allows for better organization, helps you gain as much knowledge as possible from each rapid-cycle test, and ensures that you don't skip a critical step. Let's take a look at each

step in the PDSA Cycle to better understand what will be required. Remember that each test, i.e. each PDSA Cycle, should take no longer than a few days.

Plan: In the planning stage, your goal is to make sure that your test runs as smoothly as possible, and to set up conditions that allow you to extract the most information and knowledge possible from the test. Here are some tips for a successful plan:

- Clearly define the change you are going to implement. If your plan is vague, it will likely not be implemented uniformly, and the results will be compromised. Equally important is to define the scale under which the change will be implemented. Remember, in the first test of a given change, you're only testing on a small scale, with a limited number of patients and/or staff members, so make sure that you clearly delineate who that group is.

Unclear Plan	Clear Plan
Remind clients of appointments the day before	Receptionist on the afternoon shift will make reminder calls to each client the day before his or her appointment

- Identify the staff members who will be involved, and make sure they understand exactly how the change will work, and what will be required of them during the testing period. Clearly communicate which of their responsibilities will be altered, and how, by creating a written document detailing the new method. There's no way that the staff can effectively test the change if it hasn't been clearly communicated to them.

- Determine how you will collect data, and who will collect it. Set in place a system to record the data you've decided is most relevant by assigning someone on the team to be the data-collector. Be sure the method of data collection is identical to the method you used to collect your baseline data; otherwise, your comparison may be flawed. Record data on the same form you used to record your baseline data. See Chapter 7 for information on data collection.

- Set deadlines. At the very beginning of the planning stage, make a note of the date; this is your start date. Then set a deadline: this is the end date for the test. Setting up a timeline in advance will prevent you from lingering too long on a single test. Ensure that you'll wrap things up on time by setting a date and time to meet and discuss the results of the test with the team.

- Let all staff know what you are doing. Keeping staff involved is an essential component of the NIATx model, and there can be no involvement without awareness.

- Don't get bogged down in the planning stage! Planning can be finished in one meeting with tasks assigned, data identified, dates set. Don't spend more time planning a change than doing one.

Do: In this stage you'll actually implement the change in your test, following the plan that you have created. Some points to remember:

- Set a system in place to ensure the change you're testing is being implemented correctly, exactly as you had planned, and that every staff member involved is implementing it the same way. If you are collecting a new data element, be sure that everyone who needs to is collecting it. Many a change cycle has had to be redone because one or more people forgot to collect the data.

- Record any departures from plan: If for any reason you are unable to execute the new procedure as you had planned, be sure to make a note of how things were done differently.

- Ask staff members for their input. Get their opinions about how smoothly the change is working out. Does it make their lives easier? Harder? Does it streamline the process, or does it seem to make things less efficient?

- Keep an eye on further improvement. As you go about implementing the change, think about how the change could be modified for greater improvement.

Study: Once you've executed the test and recorded relevant data, hold a meeting (the one you scheduled during the planning stage) for the team to study the results. Here, you'll analyze the outcomes of the test and figure out how to move forward.

- Compare the new data with the baseline data you collected earlier. Has the data changed? If so, in which direction has it moved? Are the results better? Worse? About the same? Creating a graph of the change in data over time will provide a helpful visual aid for understanding the information. This will help you figure out whether the change you tested seems promising.

- Start a discussion about why the outcome was the way it was. If the data show an improvement, try to pinpoint exactly what element of the process is responsible for the improvement. Could you get even more improvement by ramping up that aspect of the change? Alternatively, if the data remained the same (or turned out worse), consider why that might be—what the flaw is. After all, you decided to test a change because it seemed like a promising solution; there's a good chance that if you figure out why it didn't work, you'll be able to fix the flaw and retest with better results.

- Consider the plausibility of instituting the change on a full scale. Do you have the resources and equipment necessary to make the change into the normal procedure of your clinic? How will it affect staff workload? Will it make their work more difficult? What, if anything, will have to change besides the procedure itself? Will you have to hire more employees or add more hours? A new method may produce great results, but if it produces a negative effect on staff morale or will require heavy costs, those factors must be considered.

Act: Having digested information you gathered during the test, it's time to make some decisions about where to go from here. Generally, based on the results of the test and the plausibility concerns discussed above, there are three routes to take on a change you've tested:

1) Adopt: If the change you tested produced positive results, you'll likely want to move forward with it. Before implementing the change on a full-scale, though, it's a good idea to conduct additional rapid-cycle tests on incrementally larger scales to make sure that the improvement sticks. By moving forward in small, deliberate steps, you'll be able to confirm that the change still yields improvement if applied on a larger scale and/or under a different set of conditions. For example, if you had tested the change with four counselors, try it with eight; if you tested the change on the night shift, test it during the day shift. Sometimes by testing the change on different populations, different shifts, or different locations, you'll discover ways to streamline the new procedure or figure out in which areas it helps the most. You can also re-test a successful change in combination with another change that you've already tested individually (remember that sometimes you'll need to make more than one change to reach your improvement goals).

2) Adapt: Often the principle underlying a new procedure is solid, but it takes a few modifications before the procedure yields the desired results. If the data from the test didn't demonstrate the level of improvement you had hoped for, but you still think the change shows promise, you can adapt the change and retest it in subsequent tests. Or, even if the data exceeded your expectations, there may be a way to tweak the change to yield even greater improvements. You can also adapt a change that may have produced good results, but which seems to be unsustainable in terms of staff or resources. Use successive cycles as a way to work out the kinks in the original plan, or to refine a plan that already seems to work.

3) Abandon: When the change you've tested has failed to produce sufficient improvement and you don't see any way to adapt it to make it better, don't hesitate to walk away and go in a different direction. There's no point in trying to force a change that clearly isn't going to work, and because you've only devoted a few weeks to it, you won't fret about having wasted time. Move forward, using the knowledge that you've gained from the failed test to inform the next tests you do.

And finally: REPEAT. Keep testing changes using the PDSA Cycle, and keep trying out new ideas. By testing a change over and over, you'll get better with each test, and you'll gain more than if you had decided that your first test was good enough.

The case study that follows shows how the Acadia Hospital in Bangor, Maine used rapid-cycle testing to reduce waiting time from first call to assessment in one outpatient mental health program by more than 80 percent.

A Case Study: Rapid-Cycle Testing

About the Organization

The Acadia Hospital in Bangor, Maine, is a freestanding nonprofit psychiatric and substance abuse hospital with both inpatient and outpatient programs. It offers a range of inpatient and outpatient substance abuse and mental health treatment services for adults and children.

Aims

- Reduce waiting time to assessment in the Outpatient Mental Health Clinic serving children and adolescents

Changes

Three weeks of baseline data revealed that the average time from first call to assessment was 23.91 days, for an average of seven patients per week. The change team decided to test one change over several rapid change cycles.

PDSA Cycle 1: The first change cycle tested offering next-day appointments for clients requesting a diagnostic or treatment recommendation. To handle the appointments, the change team developed a pool of providers. This included the hospital's outpatient providers and an outside consultation and evaluation team that works throughout the Acadia Hospital system. If more clients showed up than the on-site staff could handle, they could go to another clinic onsite and be seen by a provider from the outside team. This change resulted in an almost immediate reduction in wait time.

PDSA Cycle 2: The change team combined the staff members from two departments: Ambulatory Medication Management and Intensive Outpatient/ Partial Hospital, and moved them to the same area of the building. Combining the staff allowed for crossover and help with diagnostic and treatment evaluations. This increased efficiency and enabled staff members to work at capacity, as they were rarely waiting for a no-show.

PDSA Cycle 3: Internal review of our process in this cycle uncovered a hidden problem—some providers, case managers, or pediatricians still wanted to refer clients as they had traditionally—by placing a call to talk directly to a specific psychiatrist at the clinic to arrange the referral in person. Some providers continued to want to talk to another doctor about a patient's need for diagnosis or treatment.

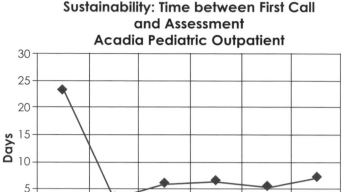

**Sustainability: Time between First Call
and Assessment
Acadia Pediatric Outpatient**

Results

As a result of this rapid-cycle test, which consisted of three distinct PDSA Cycles, wait time decreased to an average of 3.35 days, and assessments increased to 10.3 per week.

As a result of this change project, the Outpatient Mental Health clinic refined its staffing patterns in several departments to accommodate the irregular patient flow. This gave staff members a greater sense of job security.

• Collaboration and problem solving among several departments enabled the clinic to staff physician time effectively by staggering evaluation times.

• The response from providers and parents was positive, as the open access system addresses the crucial need for rapid access to help, especially for families outside the Bangor area in crisis situations.

• Rapid access to service for a child in crisis is often worth a longer drive for families who otherwise face a wait of weeks or months.

• This change helped Acadia get into the flow of a patient's care. Acadia is one part of a much bigger process of mental health service delivery, and an open access system reduces the amount of time patients, parents, and providers have to wait for the psychiatric evaluation that's essential to diagnosis and/or treatment.

Lessons Learned

1. The NIATx model made it possible to merge departments—different levels of care across different parts of the building—with the shared goal of quick access.

2. PDSA Cycles often uncover "hidden" systems—such as the physician-to-physician referral that increased patient wait time.

3. Process improvement identified what customers really wanted. Patients experiencing a level below crisis may not want or need rapid access.

This case study demonstrates how rapid-cycle testing consists of a series of PDSA Cycles conducted in quick succession. Through this series of PDSA Cycles, the Acadia Hospital change team was able to test a particular change on a small scale, identify weaknesses in it, and correct them in the next cycle. They compared the results of each change cycle to pre-test measurements to ensure that the change was actually an improvement. The change was fully implemented or "adopted" when the change cycle resulted in an improvement in the existing process.

In Summary

In rapid-cycle testing, change teams test a change through s series of PDSA Cycles. By testing a change over and over, the team gains more information about whether a change really is an improvement and ready to implement.

84

Chapter 7: Measuring Improvement: Data Collection

Data collection is an essential part of the NIATx model for process improvement, as it is data that allow you to assess your organization's current levels of performance in a particular area, set goals for improvement, and determine during testing how successful your changes are. In this section, we explain the benefits, both direct and indirect, of collecting and analyzing data, and we offer a guide to gathering and reviewing data in a simple, efficient manner.

Why Data Is Important

The NIATx model was designed to help your organization achieve specific, demonstrable goals related to one or more of the NIATx aims. It therefore follows that the progress your organization makes toward its goal should be quantifiable in some way. What does this mean, exactly? It means that you should be able to numerically measure your organization's level of performance with regard to the aim you are tackling. For this reason, it's essential that data are collected during a change project to assess whether progress is being made. In a successful change project, the data you gather and analyze will serve as evidence of the effectiveness of the change you are testing; conversely, the data will also indicate when the change being tested has failed to produce the desired level of improvement, and should thus be abandoned or adapted for retesting.

During a process improvement project, it's easy to get swept up in the excitement of developing and testing different changes. It's crucial to remember that what you are ultimately seeking is a new process that will not only be a change from the old way of doing things, but an improvement on it, leading you closer to the goal you've set out for your organization. Through data collection and analysis you can determine whether the change you are testing is actually an improvement, or if it's just a different way to get the same unsatisfactory results.

Furthermore, data collection will help you ensure that your organization continues to reap the benefits of the change after it has been implemented. By continuing to gather data once a change project is done, you can monitor performance levels to make sure that they aren't slipping; if they do begin to slip, you will know right away and will be in a position to intervene.

In addition to quantifying the impact of the changes you're testing, collecting and analyzing data can also yield several subtle benefits:

- **Definition of Goals:** Deciding what measures will serve as an indicator of improvement is useful in narrowing the scope of a change project. A clearly defined goal—say, reducing the percentage of no-shows to assessments by 35 percent—helps clarify the purpose of the project for the change team. Change projects are meant to

85

produce demonstrable progress toward a goal; defining your data can help clarify the goal.

- **Uptake:** Measuring data allows you to determine whether and how much people are using the new process.

- **Staff Support:** As you collect data, and in turn interpret that data through graphs, you will essentially translate the raw numbers into a clear illustration of the effectiveness of the changes you are testing. If a change has shown to be an improvement during testing, the data from the test can be used as evidence of the change's positive impact, which can help you gather support from staff who may be skeptical about whether the change can be implemented and what benefits it will yield. Presenting powerful visual evidence of the efficacy of the change you plan to implement can reassure staff and help bring them on board.

- **Impact Assessment:** Not all improvements are created equal. By quantifying the results of a process change, you can determine not only if it worked, but how much it worked—how big of an impact it had on performance levels. You may test several changes that seem to produce positive feedback, but unless you are tracking the data it will be difficult to determine which changes have the greatest impact for the smallest input. Knowing the level of improvement, the relative cost in terms of how much time and energy it took to achieve, and the potential benefit to the organization as well as the client, helps you sort out which changes should be adopted.

- **Insights:** One of the greatest benefits of tracking data is the unexpected insights that often arise out of a careful study of the information before you. In addition to indicating whether a change has had a positive, negative, or neutral impact on what you are trying to accomplish, an analysis of the data you collect can illuminate hidden facets of the process you are trying to improve and can generate ideas for other changes to test. Look closely at the information you have recorded. You may be able to discern patterns that allow you to identify flaws or problems in the process. From there, you can develop and test changes aimed at fixing those flaws.

The Importance of Simplicity

All this talk of data can make the process sound overwhelming and complicated, conjuring up images of pages of opaque numbers and statistics. Fortunately, such a level of complexity is not only unnecessary, but is in fact discouraged in the NIATx model. The data collection process need not and should not be overly complicated or confusing. The type of data you collect and the methods you use to collect it should be simple. In this instance, complexity is not your friend. Complex data collection methods can discourage staff, hinder the change process by making it too difficult to implement, and make it difficult to know which changes yielded an improvement. The idea isn't to accumulate as many numbers as possible; it's to collect the data that relates directly to your objective. It's important not to obscure that information or let it get lost among lots of less relevant data. Make sure any and all data you collect have a clearly defined use and purpose.

Ask yourself "What data do I need to determine whether we are making progress?" The answer should be one, or at most two, key measures.

Guidelines for Data Collection

The following is a blueprint for how to collect and interpret the data relevant to your agency's change project. Every organization's processes and goals are different, so there is no one-size-fits-all procedure. With that in mind, you may want to adjust the data collection process to meet the needs of your particular agency. Whatever you do, remember to keep it simple and not to lose sight of your aim.

Define What Constitutes Improvement and How to Measure It

Think about what you are trying to accomplish. Increasing continuation? Reducing the number of no-shows? What's the best indicator of performance level with respect to that aim? What's the best way to measure that indicator? The table on the next page gives examples of indicators you might use to measure progress toward each of the original four NIATx aims.

NIATx Aim	Indicator	How to Measure*	Improvement
Increase Admissions	Number of clients admitted in a given time frame	Count the number of clients admitted.	The number of clients admitted will increase.
Reduce No-Shows	Percentage of appointments cancelled or missed	Count the number of appointments and the number of people that showed up; then calculate the percentage of scheduled appointments that were no-shows.	The percentage of no-shows will decrease.
Reduce Wait Time	Average waiting time between first contact and first treatment session	Total the number of days waited by a set group of clients; then divide that figure by the number of clients.	The average time waited will decrease.
Increase Continuation	Percentage of clients who remain in treatment through a predetermined stage (for example, the fourth treatment session)	Select a group of clients and calculate the percentage that stayed in treatment through the predetermined stage.	The percentage of clients who remain in treatment will increase.

* Remember that you must limit the number of clients you collect data on and the timeframe for collecting data. You're trying to get data from a representative sample of clients, not every client your organization deals with.

Remember...

- In a given change project you are focusing on tackling one aim on one population at one level of care. Use those parameters when developing a definition for improvement.

- The measures you use should be agreed upon by key stakeholders, and should be clearly communicated to everyone involved in the change project.

- Eliminate ambiguity as to how you are defining your measures. If you are measuring the time elapsed between first contact and the first treatment session, will you be counting in days? In hours? What constitutes a day? It may seem self-evident, but you'll be surprised at how differently people interpret the same guidelines. It can be useful to ask several people how they would interpret the measures as you've defined them; if their answers differ, you'll want to clarify.

Develop a System for Recording the Indicator

In some cases, you may already have a system in place to record the type of data you need to evaluate your project. For example, your organization may already be making note of no-shows in an appointment log. In other cases, you may have to develop a new system to capture this information, or you may want to improve the existing system to ensure the data is recorded in an accurate, uniform, and consistent manner. In any case, you'll need to determine:

- **How** data will be collected and recorded
- **Who** will collect and record data
- **How often** the data will be reviewed
- **Who** will review the data

Think through the whole process during the planning stage to ensure that every step is accounted for, bearing in mind that gathering data is not always the same thing as recording it; it may be a two-step process. For example, you might ask a clinician to put an "X" into his or her appointment book next to each client who is a no-show for his appointment. How will those "X"'s then be counted up and recorded? How often will the numbers be recorded? Will you need to assign someone on the change team to take care of this task? Make sure that all tasks have been assigned and clearly communicated.

89

Your method of collecting data should be as simple as possible. Following are samples of forms we've developed that may be useful to you or may serve as a blueprint for developing your own forms. You can download these forms and others from the "Forms and Templates" section of www.niatx.net, Resource Center.

Referred Clients Admitted
Tracking Form

Instructions:

1. Collect baseline data for two weeks before making any changes.
2. Record a Client Identifier in Column A and the Date the Referral was Made in Column B. You will need to ask the referrer to provide this information.
3. Record the Referrer in Column C.
4. Record the Date of Admission in Column D.
5. Add comments in Column E, as needed.
6. Allow enough time to fill in the Admission Date for clients referred during the two week period.
7. What percentage of the referred clients were admitted?
   Percentage of referred clients who were admitted = # of Admissions (C) / # of Referrals (B) X 100
8. You may want to collect more information to determine at what point clients are dropping out prior to admission, for example:
   - Was a first contact made, to schedule the first face-to-face appointment?
   - Did the client show for the first face-to-face appointment?

Organization Name	
Change Being Tested	
Monday's Date	
Week # of Change Project	
Worksheet Completed by	

(A) Client Identifier	(B) Date Referral was Made	(C) Referrer	(D) Date of Admission	(E) Comments
TOTAL	# of Referrals:		# of Admissions:	

90

Visit the NIATx.net Resource Center "Forms and Templates" section to download this form.

Tracking
Reschedule Rate for No-shows

Instructions:

1. Collect baseline data for two weeks before making any changes.
2. For clients who do not show for a scheduled appointment, record a Client Identifier in Column A.
3. Record the Date of the Original Appointment to which Client Did NOT show in Column B.
4. If the client rescheduled the appointment, record the date of the rescheduled appointment in Column C.
5. Mark YES if the client showed for the rescheduled appointment in Column D. Mark NO if the client did NOT show for the rescheduled appointment.
6. At the end of the week when the next appointment was rescheduled, calculate the total number of entries in Column C and NO entries in Column D.
7. Use more pages if needed for each week.
8. What percentage of clients who did NOT show for the original appointment, reschedule:
   Reschedule Rate = # Rescheduled (C) /# No-shows to Original Appointment (B) X 100
9. What percentage of clients who rescheduled did NOT show a second time?
   No-show Rate for Rescheduled Appointments =
   # No-shows to Reschedule Appointments (D) / # Rescheduled (C) X 100

Organization Name	
Change Being Tested	
Monday's Date	
Week # of Change Project	
Worksheet Completed by	

(A) Client Identifier	(B) Date of Original Appointment to which Client Did NOT Show	(C) Date of Rescheduled Appointment	(D) Did Client Show for Rescheduled Appointment? Mark YES or NO	(E) Comments
TOTAL	# of No-shows to Original Appointment:	# Rescheduled:	# of No-shows to Rescheduled Appointment:	

91

Visit the NIATx.net Resource Center "Forms and Templates" section to download this form.

Here's an example of how you might record data on the average waiting time between first contact and the first available appointment:

Patient Name	Date of Contact	Date of Scheduled Appt.	Estimated Waiting Time (in Days)
Patient A	3/15 (A.M)	3/22 (P.M.)	8.5 Days
Patient B	3/15 (P.M.)	3/21 (A.M.)	5.5 Days
Patient C	3/15 (P.M.)	3/26 (P.M.)	11 Days
			Average: (8.5 + 5.5 + 11) / 3 = 8.3 days

Determine How You'll Express the Raw Data, and Be Consistent

There are usually several ways to express the raw data you collect. For example if you are trying to reduce no-shows, you'll be counting the number of no-shows to scheduled appointments. This information could be expressed as the percentage of appointments kept, or, conversely, the percentage of appointments missed. These are two ways to express the same information, and both are correct, but avoid confusion by making sure that you've agreed on which method of expression you'll use and make sure you are consistent.

Test your Data Collection Method with a PDSA Cycle

You'll want to make sure your data collection process works smoothly and accurately before you put it into action. One way to sort out potential problems is by doing a PDSA Cycle: Practice collecting data using the guidelines you've set up and evaluate how well the process worked. Was the right data collected? Was it collected accurately? Was there confusion about which data to record or how to record it? Did you run into unanticipated snags? Use this opportunity to correct flaws in the collection process and make sure that every step is accounted for.

Collect Baseline Data

Using the parameters already established and tested, you can begin collecting baseline data. Baseline data reveals your organization's current level of performance with regard to a particular aim, before any changes have been tested or implemented. The change leader or CEO of your organization selected a particular aim because he or she felt that the agency's performance with regard to that aim was unsatisfactory. Baseline data quantify this unsatisfactory performance; these are the numbers you are trying to improve.

In some cases, if your agency has already been (accurately) recording the necessary information as part of standard procedure, you can determine your baseline numbers by using those records. In some cases, though, you'll need to collect baseline data from scratch, using the procedure that you've developed and tested.

Collect baseline data for a short period. The time varies depending on the measure and the size of your organization, but it should be brief. If you can collect data on 10 clients in one day, you have enough data (unless that day was highly unusual). Remember that you aren't doing a research project to be published in a peer review journal—you are trying as efficiently as possible see where you are so you know how far you have to go.

Set Your Goal

Once you've collected baseline data, you can determine how your organization is currently performing with regard to your aim. For example, perhaps you tracked the number of clients who continue treatment through the fourth session and calculated that the rate of continuation is 45 percent. With that knowledge, you can set a numeric goal for what you would like to achieve with your change project. Make the goal specific—say, increasing continuation rates from 45 percent to 80 percent—and be ambitious, but be realistic, as well. Remember that you can always adjust your goal during the change project if you find, after you've begun, that your goal is too easily met or if it seems unattainable.

Develop a Graph to Illustrate Progress

As you collect baseline data and cycle through testing various changes, you'll want to compare performance levels during the phases of the change project (pre-testing, pilot testing, and the post-change sustainment period). Often, the most meaningful way to express this sort of data is through a chart or graph that allows you to compare performance over time, and see whether you are getting closer to your goal. Charts come in a number of forms. They can have an enormous visual impact and can be useful in getting the message across. The reason we use graphs is that numbers by themselves can seem abstract; many people are more comfortable with images. A visual representation of numeric data can help make the numbers easier to understand and it does a good job of illustrating changes and disparity. If you've seen an improvement in data, you'll want to choose the method that best highlights that improvement.

The chart you create should be simple, effective, and direct, and it should convey only one message. Use the X (horizontal) axis to plot time (or, if you prefer a bar graph, to plot each stage you would like to compare), use the Y (vertical) axis to plot the indicator you are measuring, and be sure to clearly identify different stages. You may want to highlight the "goal" figure to see how close you are getting with each stage.

Here's an example:

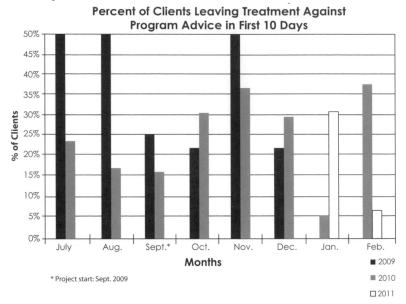

Percent of Clients Leaving Treatment Against Program Advice in First 10 Days

% of Clients

Months

* Project start: Sept. 2009

■ 2009
■ 2010
□ 2011

Remember that you'll need to assign someone with the task of periodically updating the chart and sharing it with key stakeholders in the change project.

94

Collect Data During Testing

In each PDSA Cycle you conduct, continue to collect data using the same methods you used to collect baseline data (and remember, make sure you are expressing the data in the same way). Add the data from each test you perform to the graph, and use the graph when discussing and analyzing the pilot test.

Remember to...

- Be aware of "blips" that could affect your data. For instance, a blizzard may cause a higher-than-usual number of no-shows.

- Periodically check up on the data collection and recording process to ensure it's being completed properly.

Throughout the Process, Ask Questions

What are the data telling you beyond the straightforward no-show rate, waiting time, continuation rate, or number of admissions?

Dig deeper into the process you are examining and consider other information that would be helpful to record. For example, one method of measuring no-shows is to simply make a tally mark in the appointment book next to each missed appointment. This allows you to calculate the number or rate of no-shows in a day, in a week, etc. Go a layer deeper, and you may be able to glean further useful information from your data collection. For example, you might count how many no-shows occur in the morning compared to how many no-shows occur in the evening. If the rate is heavily skewed in one direction, this may give you ideas for changes that could reduce no-shows.

This is the part of the change project that can give you real insights into the processes you are trying to improve. You already know that your organization isn't performing satisfactorily. Use the data to determine why that is, where the problem lies, and how it can be corrected. It's helpful to get multiple perspectives, so ask a few people to look at the data and offer their own interpretations and explanations—they may have different ideas and a breadth of ideas is always a good thing.

As you move forward in a change project, you may identify other relevant information that could be useful. For example, if you are trying to increase continuation rates, it may be helpful to not only record how many clients drop out of treatment, but at which stage each one drops out. That data may reveal a pattern—say, that 80 percent of dropouts happen after the first treatment session—that can show you where the problem lies and generate ideas for testing.

Be ambitious about the data you collect, and don't let any useful information go to waste. But always remember to keep it as simple as possible, and avoid combining different sets of data, as that may lead to confusion. In the example above, for instance, you would create two separate graphs to illustrate your two sets of data: one graph showing the percentage of clients who continue in treatment, and another comparing the percentage of dropouts at each stage in treatment. Always remember, one graph, one message.

The case study that follows offers a good example of the usefulness of simple data collection.

A Case Study: Data Collection

About the Organization

Ryde Drug & Alcohol Service is part of the Ryde Community Mental Health Service in New South Wales, Australia.

Aim

• Reduce no-shows to first appointments

Changes

The change team first established a proposed time frame for the project, which would begin in July 2008, wrap up in September, and be reviewed in December. The team recognized that before they could begin testing changes, they needed to determine Ryde's current rate of no-shows to first appointments. This would be the baseline data for the project.

The information needed was readily available, as Ryde clinicians had been making note of no-shows in their appointment logs as standard procedure. The team conducted a study of those logs, counting up the number of no-shows to first appointments to determine the no-show rate for each month in 2007. Then, they graphed the results:

Using the baseline data, the team determined that the overall no-show rate to first appointments in 2007 was 33 percent, although as you can see from the chart, the no-show rate fluctuated from month to month.

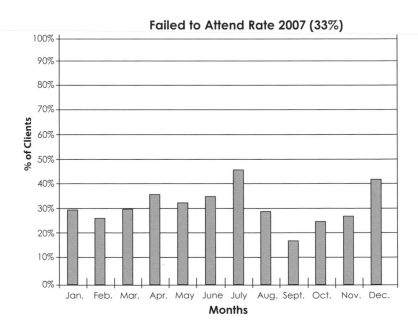

Failed to Attend Rate 2007 (33%)

% of Clients (y-axis)

Months (x-axis): Jan. Feb. Mar. Apr. May June July Aug. Sept. Oct. Nov. Dec.

To generate ideas for testing, the team held a brainstorming session to determine why so many clients were missing the first appointment. This brainstorming session produced a large number of reasons that clients had missed appointments, ranging from logistical concerns to emotional barriers to treatment. Then, the team organized all the specific reasons for no-shows into six general categories, and created a table illustrating how much each reason contributed to the overall no show rate.

Reasons for No-show

Category	Frequency	Percentage	Cumulative %
Shame/fear	9	25	25
Lack of Motivation	8	22	47
Forgot Appointment	6	17	64
Overslept	5	14	78
Comorbid Problems	4	11	89
Crisis Passed	4	11	100
Total	**36**		

Then they graphed the data from the table to provide a visual illustration of where the biggest problems lay:

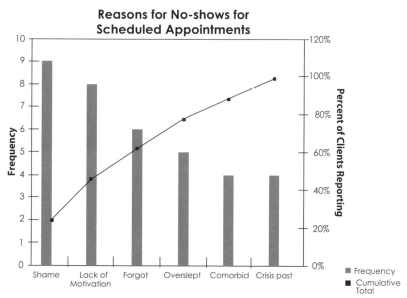

Reasons for No-shows for Scheduled Appointments

Once they understood the problem they were facing, the team decided to pilot test a new procedure for making reminder calls for first appointments. Prior to the change project, an assistant at Ryde would book appointments and write them into the clinicians' calendars—no sort of reminder was issued to clients about the appointment. The team decided to pilot test a new procedure wherein a clinician would issue a reminder call to the client prior to the client's first appointment that asked them if they planned to attend. As you can see from the graph above, the three most prominent reasons that clients weren't showing up to appointments had to do with a sense of shame, lack of motivation, or they simply forgot. The clinicians' calls helped solve each of these problems: The call served as a simple reminder about the appointment, but it also gave the clinician an opportunity to introduce herself to the client, develop a rapport, and ease the client's anxiety about beginning treatment.

They had an administrative assistant collect data on the show rate, using this log:

Appointment Scheduling Log (7/7/2008–7/9/2008)

Client Identifier	Date of Client Call	Date of Scheduled Appointment	Did Client Keep Appointment?	If CTC date of new Appointment	Did Client Keep Appointment?
1	7/2/08	7/8/08	Yes		
2	7/2/08	7/8/08	No	7/15/08	Yes
3	7/3/08	7/9/08	Yes		

After they had completed the testing period, the team graphed the results to determine whether the percentage of no-shows had dropped. Because the testing period had taken place in July/August of 2008, they included the baseline data from July/August 2007 on the graph to get a more accurate comparison and account for fluctuation throughout the year. Here's what they found.

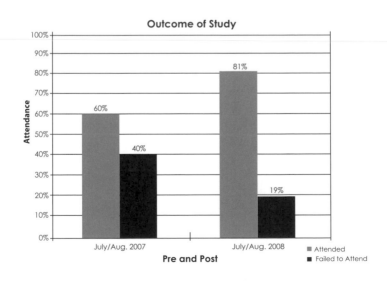

The data showed that by implementing reminder calls, Ryde had more than met its goal, reducing the no-show rate that part of the year from 40 percent to just 19 percent, a 52 percent decrease, offering demonstrable evidence of the change's success.

In Summary

By collecting data before, during, and after the change you implement, you can measure, evaluate and compare your agenciy's progress with respect to the goals you set. The process of measuring change should speed the improvement process; you should begin with simple measures rather than spending time developing a complex measuring system.

Chapter 8: Promising Practices

Experimentation is at the heart of the NIATx model. We emphasize the importance of rapid-cycle testing because short test cycles foster a "Just give it a try!" mentality, which opens up the door to all sorts of creative thinking (in addition to easing staff resistance). When brainstorming changes to test in PDSA Cycles, bold, open-minded, outside-the-box thinking can yield great results.

In this section, we present a number of strategies that your organization can use as jumping off points to generate ideas for your own change cycles. These Promising Practices, as we call them, are essentially tactics for testing that have been successful for some NIATx agencies. Some of the practices are meant to generate ideas for changes based on a certain principle, and others are a bit more specific, but all provide plenty of room for variation.

The key point here is: Make it work for you. Every organization is different: different services, different management styles and structures, different resources, and different ways of doing things—the number of variables are many. The Promising Practices we describe in this section are just some of the practices that some NIATx agencies have found to be successful. Keep in mind that what works for one agency may not work for another. Not every promising practice will be well suited to every agency, so take a critical look and think hard about which ones may be promising for your organization. If a practice doesn't seem feasible within the context of your organization, you don't have the resources to pull it off, or it sets off other alarms for you, don't use it. And if you do test a practice that doesn't seem to hold much promise for your organization, 'just consider it a learning experience and move on to the next test.

In the section that follows, we provide an overview of some of the most frequently used promising practices.

> For more detailed descriptions or to review the complete list of promising practices, visit the Promising Practices section under the Resource Center tab on www.niatx.net.

Selected Promising Practices

Remind Clients About Appointments

Aims: Reduce No-Shows, Increase Continuation

Some no-shows come about because clients simply forget their appointments. Making reminder calls a day or two prior to the appointment, be it the first appointment for a prospective client or a treatment session for a client who's already been admitted, may reduce the number of missed appointments.

101

Ideas and Tips for Testing

- Ask clients when scheduling the appointment whether they would like a reminder call; ask the best way to reach them, and whether it is all right to leave a message.

- Consider when the best time to reach clients would be—say, early evening—and make the calls then.

- During testing, select a staffer who will make the calls and create a script for the staffer to loosely follow. Keep track of how many clients you were able to reach, and whether there was a particular time of day that seemed best.

- Consider using other means of communication, such as text or e-mail. In some cases, this practice has actually resulted in higher no-show rates, so be sure to test on a small scale, making refinements as needed.

- Consider reducing no-shows to assessments and increasing continuation during treatment as two separate aims. Do separate change cycles for each. It's likely that the clients in each of those categories have different needs and concerns.

- For assessments, have the counselor make the call to begin establishing a relationship with the prospective client.

- Use the reminder call as an opportunity to ask clients about barriers they may face in making it to the appointment (see "Help Eliminate Barriers to Treatment" in the Reducing No-Shows section). Use the reminder call as an opportunity to motivate the client about treatment.

- If resources are scarce, consider making calls only to those clients who have missed appointments in the past, or identify the stage at which most drop-outs or no-shows occur and make reminder calls to clients at that stage of treatment.

For Example

Daybreak Youth Services in Spokane, Washington tested this promising practice by having one counselor make reminder calls to clients the day before their appointments, with the help of a secretary. When the practice seemed to produce a rapid improvement in no-show rates, the organization expanded it to all clinicians. In two months the clinic had reduced no-shows from 22.2 percent to 15.4 percent.

Eliminate Excessive Paperwork

Aim: Reduce Waiting Time

Redundant, overly complex, and otherwise time-consuming paperwork can take up too much time for both the client and agency' counselors and staff, significantly delaying assessments and treatment. By analyzing the paperwork required at various stages of the process and determining which information is redundant or unnecessary, and which information could be completed at a later stage, you may be able to reduce the time clients must wait.

Ideas and Tips for Testing

- The walk-through is a useful tool for identifying all the paperwork that must be completed. When walking through the paperwork, consider who fills out each form, and whether a counselor or other staff person must be present when a client fills out a form. Consider whether the volume of paperwork required might seem overwhelming to prospective clients.

- Separate the forms the client can complete on his own from the forms that he must complete with a counselor present. Redesign the process to ensure that the counselor is only present when she needs to be. For forms that currently require a counselor's presence while the client fills them out, consider whether a nonclinical staffer could take on the role.

- Eliminate redundant information between forms.

- Don't mistakenly eliminate forms that are required by law or are otherwise mandatory.

- Put off getting information from a client until the information is actually needed.

- If paring down the paperwork seems overwhelming, consider doing separate change cycles to address paperwork at each step of the treatment process (pre-assessment, assessment, treatment, etc.).

- Ensure that the time saved by streamlining the paperwork is put to good use. Come up with a plan for how to use that time—for example, additional assessments.

(103)

- During rapid-cycle testing, collect data on how much time staff and clients spend on the required paperwork. Make note of whether the redesigned paperwork allowed counselors and staff to access information as needed.

For Example

Iowa's Community and Family Resources realized that taking a client's psychosocial history during the assessment was a waste of time if clients weren't recommended for treatment. By delaying taking the history until after the client had been admitted, they were able to shave a full hour off the assessment, which in turn helped to reduce the waiting time for treatment from 39 days to 4 days.

Use the Spirit of Motivational Interviewing During First Contact

Aim: Reduce No-Shows

Just as some clients face logistical barriers in getting to appointments, others may face emotional barriers, such as reluctance to change or not feeling ready for treatment that may cause them to skip appointments. Using motivational interviewing (a method designed to help someone resolve his or her ambivalence about change) during first contact can help engage and reassure the client.

Ideas and Tips for Testing

- Ask open-ended questions and show empathy with the prospective client's situation and concerns.

- Recognize the reasons clients may be resistant to treatment.

- Explain how treatment can help them address specific goals they'd like to achieve or problems they'd like to overcome.

- Show that you've been listening by summarizing what the client has said.

- Encourage referrers to use motivational interviewing when referring clients to your agency.

- During testing, create a script for a chosen staff member to use during first contact with clients. Ask the staff member to practice the script until he or she feels comfortable improvising.

- When evaluating the pilot test, consider how easy or difficult the staffer felt it was to use MI techniques, whether he felt it was useful, and any changes that could be made to the guidelines.

For Example

By asking open-ended questions during first contact to determine what the client wanted to get out of treatment, and then discussing ways to meet those needs, California's PROTOTYPES reduced no-shows to the first in-person outpatient appointment from 36 percent to 10 percent.

104

Offer More Groups Instead of Individual Sessions

Aim: Reduce Waiting Time

In some cases, an agency may be assigning clients to individual appointments when they could, in fact, be seen in groups. By offering group sessions instead of individual sessions, counselors will be able to see more clients in the same period.

Ideas and Tips for Testing

- Keep in mind that counselors will need to expend more energy on group sessions than individual sessions, and schedule accordingly.

- Consider creating group assessment appointments that include an informational video that the group views together, as well as brief private assessments.

- Add group treatment sessions.

- During rapid-cycle testing, pay attention to whether group sessions allowed counselors to provide an appropriate level of care.

For Example

Orlando's Center for Drug Free Living began using a group format for the initial assessment instead of individual appointments, which decreased the waiting time for treatment from 24 days to 8 days, and increased the number of assessments per month from 43 to 52.

Centralize Appointment Scheduling

Aim: Reduce Waiting Time

When counselors spend too much time scheduling appointments, they have less to spend with clients. Eliminate this waste of resources by establishing a centralized system for making appointments that doesn't require counselor involvement.

Ideas and Tips for Testing

- Consider scheduling appointments on electronic calendars that can be shared by counselors and administrative staff.

- Discuss with counselors any concerns they might have about sharing their appointment books, and win support by testing the change on a small scale.

- Use the new scheduling system both for patients scheduling on the phone and those scheduling in person.

For Example

Sinnissippi Centers in Illinois increased revenues from assessments by 60 percent by centralizing appointment scheduling to the front desk.

(105)

Combine multiple intake and assessment appointments

Aim: Reduce Waiting Time

By combining the intake, assessment, evaluation, and admission processes into one single appointment (or as few appointments as possible), clients can get into treatment sooner.

Ideas and Tips for Testing

- Wait to collect information from clients until the information is actually needed.

- Redesign the assessment process so that it requires only a single visit.

- During testing, consider whether a single-visit assessment provides sufficient care for the client.

- Use the testing opportunity to look for inefficiencies in the intake process (such as redundant paperwork).

For Example

By combining the evaluation and intake appointments of clients that clearly met the requirements for admission, Connecticut Renaissance in Bridgeport was able to reduce average waiting time between evaluation and intake from 21 days to 6 days.

Adjust staff schedules to meet client demand

Aims: Reduce Waiting Time, Reduce No-Shows, Increase Continuation

Determining the specific needs of your clients with regard to scheduling allows you to adjust staff schedules to meet these needs, making appointments more convenient for clients and thus getting more clients through in less time. For example, if many of your clients work day jobs, it makes sense to offer more appointments in the evening to accommodate their work schedules. This practice, which ultimately makes it more convenient for clients to make it to appointments, can also reduce no-shows and increase continuation.

Ideas and Tips for Testing

- Ask appointment-making staff to note what times of day clients frequently request appointments. This will give you an idea of when demand is highest, and you can increase time slots during that time.

- When evaluating your change during testing, consider whether you chose the right time slots to add.

- Determine whether there's a particular time of day when the no-show rate is higher or lower than normal and use this knowledge when deciding when to add slots.

For Example

Salt Lake City's Cornerstone Counseling Center reduced the average waiting time between first contact and assessment from 13 to 4 days by providing Friday assessments for any client not assessed earlier in the week, thus assuring that all clients could be assessed within a week of first contact.

Establish walk-in hours

Aims: Reduce Waiting Time, Reduce No-Shows

Creating time-slots when prospective clients can see counselors without having made an appointment allows more clients to get into treatment and reduces the time that counselors would have wasted on no-shows.

Ideas and Tips for Testing

- Have backup counselors on hand in case there are not enough staff scheduled to accommodate the demand for services.

- Start by testing the change on a small scale to gauge client interest in walk-in hours.

- Add walk-in hours in small increments so as not to overwhelm staff.

- Estimate how many walk-ins you expect to get and assign the appropriate number of counselors and staff; adjust and retest based on how many walk-in clients you actually receive.

- Publicize your new walk-in hours with referral sources.
- Don't turn away walk-in clients.
- During testing, compare the number of clients assessed during walk-in hours to the number of assessments that typically would have taken place during that time.
- Take care in considering which block of time to use for walk-in hours.
- Clearly outline the walk-in policy and communicate the policy to staff and counselors.

For Example
Southwest Florida Addiction Services created a total of 16 walk-in hours each week, increasing the number of assessments per month from 112 to 122, as well as reducing the waiting time for assessments from 35 days to 7 days.

Orient Clients
Aims: Reduce No-Shows, Increase Continuation, Increase Admissions
Clients often enter treatment (or a new level of care) with a great deal of anxiety, in part because they don't know what to expect. Orienting clients to treatment or to a new level of care before they begin helps ease this anxiety.

Ideas and Tips for Testing

- Consider creating a script for orientation during first contact.
- Consider the possibilities of creating a video orientation.
- Create documents that let the clients know what to expect.
- Use counselors from the next level of care or alumni to orient clients.

Follow up with No-shows
Aims: Reduce No-Shows, Increase Continuation
By following up with a no-show to determine why she missed her appointment, you can reschedule an appointment, re-engage the client, and identify barriers that clients face that your organization may be able to remedy.

Ideas and Tips for Testing

- Use the follow-up call to help the client overcome the barrier(s) that prevented him from getting to his appointment and ensure that he will make it to his rescheduled appointment.
- Consider the barriers that clients mention and consider changes your agency could make to eliminate them.
- Start following up with clients after the first missed appointment, thus making them aware that their absence is noticed.

- Have counselors make the follow-up calls, using the opportunity re-engage the client in treatment.

- Start calling clients 10 or 15 minutes after their scheduled appointment time if they haven't shown up.

- Follow up with clients who cancel assessments without rescheduling.

- Use separate change cycles for following up with no-shows to assessments and no-shows who have already begun treatment, as these two categories of clients will likely have different needs, barriers, and concerns.

- When evaluating the test, consider both how many clients rescheduled during the follow-up, and how many showed up for the rescheduled appointment.

For Example

In Orlando, The Center For Drug Free Living had counselors make follow-up calls to outpatient clients who missed their first appointment. The calls were made within 24 hours of the missed appointment and resulted in 70 percent of those clients returning to treatment and completing at least four sessions.

Identify Clients at Risk for Leaving and Intervene

Aim: Increase Continuation

 Getting feedback from clients helps you better identify those who seem to be at risk of leaving, allowing you to find a solution to keep them engaged in treatment.

Ideas and Tips for Testing

- During testing, develop a method for getting feedback from clients, such as a questionnaire assessing their feelings about the program and their level of motivation to stay in treatment. Adjust and refine your methods as you retest.

- Develop a method for counselors and staff to communicate their concerns about clients at risk for leaving, and share thoughts on how to intervene.

- Use PDSA Cycles to test and refine different methods of intervening (such as motivational interviewing) when a client seems to be at risk.

- Study at which stages clients tend to drop out of treatment, and be attentive to clients during those stages. Consider the needs of clients at that stage when brainstorming ways to intervene.

- Weekly reviews using the Session Rating Scale or a personalized tool developed for your agency can identify those clients most at risk.

For Example

Bridge House in New Orleans instituted a questionnaire that each week asked clients to rate on a scale of 1–10:

- How willing are you to continue treatment here?
- How important is it for you to stay in treatment?
- How motivated are you to stay?
- How strong has your urge to use been this past week?

They also implemented weekly meetings for counselors to discuss continuation issues and ways to intervene with at-risk clients, used Motivational Interviewing techniques to re-engage those clients, and planned one specific change to motivate each client and assessed its efficacy using PDSA cycles. As a result, continuation rates jumped from 48 percent to 63 percent.

Offer a Tour Guide

Aims: Increase Continuation, Increase Admissions
Clients and family who are overwhelmed by the idea of navigating the treatment process may benefit from interactions with a tour guide whom the client can relate to, and who can help guide him through treatment.

Ideas and Tips for Testing

- Peers in recovery may serve as tour guides for new clients.
- Assign tour guides to keep track of a client's funding and benefits so that they don't' expire before he or she is ready to move to the next level of care.
- Have the tour guide meet with clients before discharge to map out the transition to outpatient care.
- After discharge, arrange for the client to meet with his or her tour guide for several weeks to aid in the transition period.
- With regard to covering the tour guide's salary, remember that some providers can bill tour guide hours directly as case management or social work; others are able to increase the billable hours of case managers.
- During testing, get feedback from clients about how they felt about having a tour guide.
- During testing, experiment with different levels of interaction between client and tour guide.

For Example
To increase continuation from the hospital to outpatient care, the Partnership for Advancing Recovery of Kentucky appointed "family health navigators" who visit with clients to encourage continuation, and get them into aftercare at the community provider level. Continuation increased from about 28 percent to 52 percent.

Many treatment organizations face the possibility of losing a reliable source of revenue—for example, a block grant from the state or county. One remedy for that situation is to increase the number of referrers who send you fee-for-service clients—clients who can self-pay or who have insurance coverage. Follow these steps to increase targeted admissions:

Ten Steps to Increase Targeted Admissions

① Identify Referrers

Identify existing sources of referrals to your outpatient program. Referrers send you clients who are either starting treatment, or transitioning from another level of care. Referrers that start clients in treatment include:

- The client (self-referral)
- Family and friends
- Employers
- Schools
- Your staff
- Other healthcare providers (e.g., emergency departments, physicians, etc.)
- Child protective services
- Welfare agencies
- Judges, lawyers, and probation officers
- Faith community

Referrers that transition clients into outpatient care from another level of care include:

- Detoxification centers
- Residential treatment
- Inpatient rehabilitation
- Partial hospitalization
- Intensive outpatient treatment

Referrals between levels of care can be within your own agency, or external—between your agency and an outside organization.

② Invite One Referrer to Join You

Start with one referrer and learn how to improve that one referral process. Improvements for one referrer can usually be spread to other, similar referrers. Invite the first referrer based on the referrer's ability to:

- Lead you to payers who pay more for more outpatient admissions. Not all payers will pay more. Some place annual caps on the amount they will pay you. Use the entire amount—or risk having it reduced even further. Then, either renegotiate a higher cap, or select payers who will pay more for more outpatient admissions.

- Offer a large number of admissions. Working jointly with a referrer, especially if it is another organization, is time consuming no matter how well it is done. Make it worthwhile. A detox program, probation office, or residential program may actually be referring more clients than you know. The clients may be referred but never make it to admission.

- Make appropriate referrals. Ensure that the referrer is in a position to refer clients who will be physically located in your geographic area when discharged from another level of care and ready to begin outpatient treatment.

- Easily work together. Increasing internal transitions within the same organization is usually easier than working with two different organizations.

- Work with you in the past. It is easier to work together if you already share a history of joint problem solving.

- Participate in making improvements. Payers (both private and public) have an interest in making sure their payment for one level of care is not lost or repeated because of a failed transition to another level of care. They will often join you and participate on a Change Team devoted to increasing the number of admitted referrals to demonstrate successful outcomes.

- Others—there are always other good reasons.

Referrers will have their own reasons for joining a change team. Increasing your admissions is not their problem. However, they have problems that this joint effort may solve. Consider using Motivational Interviewing when you approach the referrer.

If it is a starting referral, the referrer may want outpatient care to meet conditions for:

- Reduced jail time
- Probation
- Keeping a driver's license
- Readmission to school
- Continued employment
- Access to children
- A continued relationship
- Treatment for a co-occurring mental health disorder
- Others—use whatever reasons work to get addiction treatment started

If it is a transition referral, the referrer may want to:

- Improve their outcomes (they know that without transitioning clients to outpatient care, the clients are more likely to relapse)

- Transition clients to a lower, more appropriate level of care (especially if the payer denies payment for inappropriate placement of clients)

- Free up space for the waiting list by transitioning appropriate clients to outpatient treatment

- Make sure the client transitions within your own organization instead of to another, competing program

- Others—there are always other reasons. Use whatever reasons work to engage the referrer in the Change Project.

③ Form a Joint Change Team

Include change leaders from both the referring organization and your outpatient program and make sure the executive sponsors from both organizations sign off on the charter. If you decide to work with self-referrals (where there is no referral organization), be sure to add someone who can represent the client's perspective such as alumni to your change team. Adding someone who represents the client's perspective is always a good idea; if self-referrals are the selected referral source, it is essential.

④ Invite the Referrer to Participate in a Walk-through

Jointly walk through the referral process to experience the transition from a client's perspective. Ask two people, preferably the change leaders from both the referring organization and the outpatient agency, to walk through the referral process together. Walk through both organizations' referral processes to experience the referrer's hand off and the outpatient program's reception and admission of the client.

⑤ Agree on Aims

After completing the walk-through, jointly agree on an aim for the project. For example, the aim might be to increase the number of referrals who are admitted to your outpatient program. The referrer will have their reasons for joining the change team. However, you and the referrer need to agree on the aim for this project and both executive sponsor s need to approve it.

⑥ Establish Baseline Data

To establish a baseline, count the number of referrals made by the referrer, and the number of referrals who are admitted. This may require manual data collection for a few weeks:

- The referrer tracks the number of clients referred. With client permission, the referrer may even contact the outpatient program to alert you to a potential admission.

- The outpatient program tracks the number of referred clients who are admitted.

⑦ Identify Barriers and Opportunities

Use the results of the walk-through to identify problems and opportunities in the referral process in both organizations. Assume that problems are never the fault of the client, but of the process itself. Even if you don't believe this, act as if it is never the client's fault. The referral process can always be improved to the point where almost all transition referrals end with the client being admitted to the next level of care.

⑧ Test Promising Practices

Test NIATx promising practices (visit www.NIATx.net "Provider Toolkit") to improve the referral process. It is unlikely that only one promising practice will increase the number of referrals who are admitted; test more than one to find out which is most effective for your organization.

⑨ Sustain Improvements

Seventy percent of process improvements—in all fields—don't survive past six months. That being the case, you can safely assume that increased referrals and admissions won't survive either unless you make efforts to sustain the improvements that you have made.

- Use what you have learned from your clients who stay in recovery. Sustaining improvement is an ongoing process that never ends. Like recovery, a process improvement is not a one-time event and relapse—or reverting back to the old way of doing things--is not necessarily a sign of failure. Relapse is part of most improvement projects and can be a positive experience when it shows that additional changes are required to sustain the improvement.

Sustainable improvements are:

- Impossible to remove
- Make the staff's job easier
- Based on a strong business case
- Subject to continuous monitoring
- Assigned the necessary resources

⑩ Invite another Referrer to Join You

With the experience you've gained working with one referrer to increase admissions, you're ready to invite other referral sources to join you to increase the number of their referrals that end in an admission. Return to Step 3.

For example:
St. Christopher's Inn in Garrison, New York generated an additional $1,400,000 in revenue by attracting additional referral sources. The Administrative Director of Counseling and Shelter Services, who was also the change leader, developed relationships with labor

assistance professionals to increase referrals through labor union employee assistance programs and to meet their specific needs. He worked with private insurance companies to be "in-network" and negotiated a better payment rate. The payer mix for private insurance increased from 7 percent to 15 percent. St. Christopher's Inn also tracked trends in referrals from existing referral sources to identify additional referral sources to work with, resulting in an additional $100,000 per year. They secured an additional contract with the New York State Division of Parole, adding $110,000 per year.

In Summary

Remember that the NIATx Promising Practices are not meant to serve as direct instructions; rather, they are meant to serve as jumping off points to help you generate your own ideas for testing that are best suited to your organization's needs. As you read through the Promising Practices, ask yourself "How can I make this practice, or the basic idea behind this practice, work for my organization?" Think of the practices as fluid ideas that can be adapted and shaped around the specific attributes of your agency. Be flexible, and use what you know about your own organization to develop ideas for change that will work for you.

Chapter 9: Looking Outside the Field

Creative thinking is integral to the NIATx model, and we encourage you to think outside the box when brainstorming changes to test. One important element of this (so important, in fact, that we made it one of the five NIATx principles) is looking to industries outside your field for ideas and practices that can be applied in one form or another in the treatment setting. There is much to be learned from the successes of businesses in other industries, and there is no reason that the practices that work for them cannot be creatively reshaped to allow your organization to be more successful.

Compare any two industries, no matter how different they may seem, and you'll almost always be able to find parallels and commonalities. No matter what the objective of your process improvement project might be, if you look hard enough and think creatively enough, you'll discover that other businesses have comparable objectives, or that the challenges they face are similar to the ones that you face. Examining the strategies and practices that these businesses have put in place to achieve those objectives or to overcome those challenges can help you generate creative ideas for pilot testing, whether they're nearly identical to those practices that have worked for other businesses or inspired by them.

Why Look to Other Fields

One reason that looking outside the field can be helpful is that during the course of a change project, you'll likely come up with a number of objectives related to the larger aim of the project with which you have little experience and don't know how to initiate. However, there is likely another industry for whom achieving that same objective is an essential part of their business model and, thus, something they've already developed successful strategies to deal with. What this means is that if you can identify these cases, you can adapt the experience and knowledge of other companies to your advantage.

To illustrate this point, imagine that, in an effort to increase admissions, you decide to explore ways of getting the word out to referral agencies about the services your organization offers, accomplishments you are proud of, etc. Publicity isn't a treatment agency's primary concern, and it likely isn't something you know much about or are particularly skilled in. However, there's a whole industry devoted solely to publicity, and there are numerous tried-and-true, time-tested strategies employed by any good publicist. These practices are employed because publicists know they work. So when you're trying to attract the attention of referral sources, you'd do well to steal some tips from the masters. What could you learn from the way they operate? Publicists maintain meticulous databases with up-to-date contact information of people and businesses that they market products to. They don't only keep records of the main contact number for a company they're marketing to, but the specific person at that business who would be most interested in the product, and they keep their databases categorized by type of markets.

Furthermore, a good publicist would send customized press releases to different types of publications, tailored to fit that publication's audience. In essence, they put time and effort into figuring out what information to send and to whom to send it. Knowing how a publicist operates lets you borrow some of their practices and use them for your own purposes. And remember, you don't need to adopt all their practices—you might find that it makes a big difference simply to learn the name of the person at a referral agency who would be most interested in your organization's services, so you know to whom to address promotional materials.

There is really no limit to what you can learn from the strategies and practices of other industries provided you are willing to think creatively about how they can be related to your own organization.

Brainstorming Strategies

Although the possibilities are nearly endless, they aren't always immediately apparent, so it's worth your time to try to develop brainstorming skills that will allow you to find the parallels between two different businesses.

Because you're looking for parallels, and not equivalents, it can be helpful to start by thinking in more abstract terms; i.e., think of the bigger concept, not the details. For example, you might think of an ice cream truck. What is the fundamental principle behind its services, and what makes it valuable to its customers? Unlike, say, an ice cream store, the ice cream truck goes to its customers rather than requiring the customers to come to it. The products offered are listed on the side of the truck, and ice cream trucks make their presence known in a neighborhood, often by playing music.

Now think of how these principles could be applied in a reasonable way to your agency. How could you bring your services to the customer? Although you may not offer treatment services from a truck (though some agencies do), perhaps you could create a neighborhood event and set up a booth where people could get information about your services, and even set up appointments. You could create signage that broadcasts the services you offer, and put up fliers around the neighborhood in advance to raise awareness of the event.

Remember to think big, as in be creative, but also small—often success is found in the details, and making smaller changes inspired by the practices of other industries have just as big an impact as appropriating a large-scale practice (and will likely be easier to test and implement).

To illustrate how a brainstorming session would work, here are some notes from a 2006 NIATx workshop called "The Improvement Café." Led by NIATx coaches, the group took a hard look at how one aspect of the restaurant industry operates, and brainstormed which strategies used by restaurants could be adapted for use in the substance abuse treatment field.

Rather than taking on all the practices of the restaurant industry, they looked at a narrow slice of how restaurants operate: how they seat their customers and turn over tables. This is only one element of running a restaurant, but it's a good one to look at because it's something that a restaurant must do well to be successful, and therefore it's something that successful restaurants have put a lot of time and effort into perfecting.

The group posed the question, "If your organization were a restaurant, how would you seat your customers?" Here is what they came up with:

- **Advertise immediate seating.** Let clients know that they can have immediate access through on-demand treatment or walk-in appointments.

- **Schedule by demand.** Restaurants add staff to accommodate greater demand at peak times—before or after a sold-out cultural or sporting event. Treatment organizations can adopt the same practice to meet demand at peak times.

- **Offer a drive-through window.** Treatment organizations can offer express service for clients who want quick access to information: the organization's important phone numbers, insurance coverage options, transportation and childcare services, or a directory of local Twelve-Step meetings.

- **Publish menu options in the Yellow Pages or online.** Listing your organization's offerings similar to a restaurant's carryout or delivery menu in the local Yellow Pages increases your customers' access to information about your services—and could influence no-shows.

- **Create a comfortable waiting area.** Would you rather stand in line for a table at a popular restaurant or take a seat in a comfortable lounge area listening to music or watching TV? Treatment organizations can offer their clients a pleasant and relaxing place to sit while they wait for an appointment.

- **Establish a turnover team.** Busy restaurants employ staff to clear and set tables as they turn over. A turnover team at a residential treatment organization would be able to keep staff notified of up-to-the-minute bed availability and make sure the room is ready for a new patient.

As you can see, many of the restaurant industry's strategies for seating customers can be adapted to help get clients into and out of treatment efficiently.

Learning from the Best

When it comes to looking to other industries for practices that can be incorporated into the treatment setting, it's difficult to know where to start—where to look, and what to look for. One place to begin is by identifying what you are trying to do, and thinking about which industries and even specific companies are successfully doing the same thing, or something similar or analogous. Then ask yourself, "Which business or businesses do it best? What makes them so good?" Once you've identified who does this particular thing best, you can

(117)

analyze how they operate to isolate the reasons why they are successful and adapt those practices to suit your organizational needs.

To illustrate how this principle might work, let's look at some objectives that your organization might take on and think about which other industries share those objectives, which of them excel at accomplishing them, how they do it, and how their methods might be adapted for your own purposes.

For this exercise, we use as our objectives some of the requisite components that NIATx has determined to be essential to any redesigned treatment system. Here, we'll take a few of these "essential ingredients," as we call them, and discuss how you might incorporate them into a treatment agency by using the knowledge and experience of other industries.

Essential Ingredients

At NIATx, we wanted to determine what concepts—not specific practices, but rather larger tenets—were essential to redesigning a treatment system that really addressed the needs of the customer and that delivered the best care possible.

To do so, we first gathered a group of people affected by or involved in substance abuse treatment, such as users, their family members, treatment providers, and workers in the criminal justice system. Using interviews and Nominal Group Technique (NGT) sessions (see Chapter 4 for more information on NGT), we asked the participants to identify the greatest barriers they faced in their respective roles. After compiling and prioritizing the list of barriers, we convened a meeting of 12 individuals, some from within the substance abuse industry and some from outside of it whose insights we believed would be valuable additions to the discussion (the parent of a user, for example, and a quality improvement coach). Through extensive discussion and assessment, the group identified 11 fundamental tenets that we determined to be essential in any substance abuse treatment system that would successfully address the barriers that our participants had identified. These "essential ingredients" are:

- Anytime/anywhere direct-to-consumer assessment, treatment, and continuing care

- Minimal variation in the quality of assessment, treatment, and continuing care

- Use of emerging and existing technologies

- Global assessment, treatment, and continuing care of patient (and family) needs and assets

- Soft and minimal handoffs

- Evidence-based practices

- Connecting, supporting, and engaging patients, families, peers, and providers before, during, and after treatment

- Offering just-in-time continuing care, ongoing monitoring with as-needed outreach, skill development, preventive intervention, social support, and emergency response to derail crises

- Providing mechanisms to help the patient and family recover in a hostile environment

- Using valid, timely, and practical progress measures

- Pay for performance

We describe a few of these essential ingredients below.

Anytime/Anywhere Direct-to-Customer Assessment, Treatment, and Continuing Care

In our world, this means providing care to clients when they need it and where they need it. This type of service is critical in a field where timing and accessibility can be crucial to recovery.

It's also an idea that's used in a variety of other industries, and is often an integral part of their business model. On the spot, 24/7 service is an amenity that many businesses have incorporated, to great effect. What businesses can you think of that have perfected the art of 24/7 service? Consider, for example, a hotel concierge service that can bring the guest whatever he might need, at any time, with just a phone call. Or, in a completely different application of the same idea, think of emergency services like 911. What can you learn from these examples?

One method is to examine what these services have in common. Both must not only be capable of providing their service at all times, but they must also be reachable at all times, which means that they must have a phone line that is staffed by an actual person at all hours to respond to callers.

Now, think of how this principle might be applied in the treatment setting. You could follow this example and institute a hotline that's always staffed and ready to take calls from clients in need, or their friends or family to help them through a crisis. Even if you are unable to provide care 24/7, you might still consider implementing a 24-hour phone line staffed by someone who can help callers figure out how to get the care they need at that moment. It's important to remember to assess which elements of a particular practice are plausible for your purposes, which aren't, and how a practice that might be implausible can be adapted to meet your needs.

Soft and Minimal Handoffs

As we discussed in Chapter 3, handoffs are a delicate part of the treatment continuum, and their success is critical to continuation.

Handoffs and transitions happen in all kinds of industries in a variety of forms. In fact, handoffs provide a great example of how you can use the success of other businesses because there are so many types of handoffs to consider and thus many strategies and tactics that can be adapted for the treatment process.

Start by defining what a handoff is, in a broad sense: the physical transfer of an object (in this case, a person) from one domain to another, as well as the transfer of responsibility for that object from one authority to another. When you think about it that way, in general terms, you'll begin to see how many analogous situations exist outside the substance abuse treatment industry.

For example, think about air traffic controllers. As a plane flies, it passes through several regions of authority, each coordinated by a different air traffic controller. An air traffic controller is responsible for a plane as soon as it enters the air space under her authority; as it moves into the next air space, she transfers responsibility to the air traffic controller responsible there. The stakes here are high, and perfection is critical.

Handing off planes is different from handing off clients between levels of care, but consider how air handoffs happen, and what you could learn from them. How might they differ from a handoff at a treatment facility? How might they be the same? One thing you might notice is the border between regions of authority is clearly defined; responsibility is transferred directly from one controller to the next, and at no time is the plane unsupervised by air traffic control. This might seem obvious—of course we don't' want planes flying around without supervision and coordination. But that scenario is similar to what often happens when a client moves from one level of care to another.

When clients are discharged from one level of care and are responsible for getting themselves to the next level, they are often unaccompanied, unsupervised, and uncared for. In this case, you could take a tip from air traffic controllers and institute a policy by which a client who is ready to move on is personally "delivered" to the new level of care by personnel from the previous level. This creates a clearly delineated transfer of responsibility, allows for face-to-face communication between the "delivering" and "receiving" personnel, and ensures that there is no gap in care.

Furthermore, an air traffic controller receives a plane's updated flight information before the plane comes under her authority, ensuring at the moment the plane becomes her responsibility, she is prepared. How could this principle of preparing for the transfer be applied in the treatment handoff process?

Or, to consider an example of a different type of handoff in a different industry, think about high-end spas, which often employ a staff person whose sole job is to greet clients and to lead them from one treatment to the next, and to make sure all their needs are being met. Being greeted, picked up after one treatment, and delivered to the next all by the same person provides continuity for the client, making sure that the client is never lost or unsure of where to go, and making the client feel cared for. How might this practice be adapted for treatment handoffs?

Connecting, Supporting, and Engaging Patients, Families, Peers, and Providers Before, During, and After Treatment

Building a support network for clients and their families that facilitates entry into treatment and that remains in place post-treatment is key, but it's difficult to maintain this type of engagement, especially once the client has left treatment. What types of businesses have created strong networks of support for their clients (and families)? One answer might be universities that create support networks for students and their families that extend well beyond graduation.

Generate a list of all the steps universities take to create and maintain social networks: Many colleges organize get-togethers for incoming students and their families before the school year begins so that the students can meet each other and ease the adjustment. Some colleges have parents associations. And most colleges have a strong, well-tended, and well-staffed alumni network that allows the school to keep up to date with what alums are doing, and in turn to let them know the happenings on campus, often via regular alumni magazines or newsletters. Furthermore, many universities have special web pages for alumni, who can sign in and keep in touch with one another or make professional connections. And of course, colleges hold reunions and other types of get-togethers for graduates. Which of these strategies might be adapted to work for behavioral health programs? Holding regular social events for "graduates" and their families? Offering pre-treatment groups for those who are not quite ready to enter into treatment?

Mechanisms to Help the Patient and Family Recover in a Hostile Environment

Substance abuse treatment agencies provide the client with a safe space where he can work on recovering without distractions or negative influences. However, there comes a time when the client must leave treatment and return to the "real world," which can be a dangerous, hostile place that makes it difficult to maintain a healthy lifestyle.

Where else do people typically encounter hostile environments, and what support is put in place to help them? One industry in which people are regularly placed in dangerous or hostile environments is the police force, where officers constantly find themselves in antagonistic situations. One strategy that the police force uses to counteract this hostility and to protect its officers is to always work in pairs, so that each has a partner to count on for protection, help, and back up.

Could that basic idea work for clients emerging from treatment? Would it be possible to pair up departing clients as they go back to their lives? A partner back in the real world who is experiencing the same thing and knows what it's like could perhaps provide positive emotional support and advice, and could step in if she feels that her partner is going to relapse.

In Summary

As you can see there are many possibilities for getting ideas from outside the field. Think about your own great and terrible experiences with various service providers and identify what makes them great or not so great. Look at companies that are at the top of their industry and think about why they are at the top. This kind of thinking will help you start to identify ideas from outside the field that you can adapt for use in your own organization.

Chapter 10: Common Barriers

One important part of process improvement is troubleshooting. The ability to recognize, diagnose, and overcome barriers to progress is an essential skill for any organization that wishes to create a culture of improvement. In many cases, the most difficult aspect of troubleshooting is not solving the problem, but identifying it in the first place. In this chapter, you'll find information on some of the most common barriers encountered during NIATx change projects, the possible causes and symptoms of these barriers, and tips for overcoming them.

Few problems exist independently; that is to say, barriers are often interconnected, with one causing another. Several barriers may result from a single underlying cause. Furthermore, often the perceived "problem" in a change project is actually a symptom of a deeper issue. In such cases, putting the project back on track requires working backward to discover the root of the problem.

With this in mind, for each barrier mentioned in this chapter we've included other barriers that may be related, whether as causes or as symptoms. Use these lists as aides to help you identify the problem and diagnose the root cause. Then you can use our problem-solving tips to overcome those barriers and move forward successfully.

1. The Problem: The Project Is Dragging on Too Long

Change projects are not meant to be open ended—they are meant to move quickly and efficiently in order to extract the maximum benefits. A project that is dragging on is likely a sign of an underlying problem.

Possible Causes: Staff resistance; diminishing enthusiasm; insufficient time for testing; team is lost; team members are not being held accountable; project is unmanageable; change leader does not feel empowered to make decisions; the team is not generating ideas; ineffectual change leader; lack of communication and meetings

The Fix: Head off this problem from the start by establishing a solid time frame for the project before you even begin. Plan out the start date for a project and for each change cycle in the project, and set a finite completion date, taking care to be specific ("sometime early next year" does not count as a completion date). Setting deadlines can help create a sense of urgency that can motivate the team to keep things moving.

In the event that you find your team in the middle of a never-ending project, try to diagnose the root cause of the lack of progress to determine where things went off track, and be sure to consider the other possible causes discussed in this chapter.

2. The Problem: Staff Resistance

Possible causes: There are a number of reasons why staff might be resistant to a particular change, or the change project as a whole. Some possibilities:

- Concern that the change will increase workloads

- Skeptical that the change can be successfully implemented

- Skeptical that the change will yield improvement

- Not understanding why the process needs to be improved

- So settled into the status quo that they have a general fear of changing the routines and processes they are accustomed to

The Fix: If you understand the reason for resistance, you'll be in a better position to overcome it. As you are trying to gain staff support, think of the staff as your customers, and remember the first principle of the NIATx model: Understand the needs of the customer. Try to understand where your staff is coming from, and how they will be affected by the change. Do they have reason to be concerned? Being aware of how a change will affect the staff's workload as you develop and test the process can help you avoid overburdening the staff and making their jobs more difficult.

First, engage staff in identifying possible solutions through the nominal group process. People don't like change that's imposed on them; they are less reluctant to engage in change that they have chosen. Also, be clear about the pilot testing process. Nothing that is ineffective will be implemented.

124 In most organizations, staff have experienced a lot of ineffective change. Early in the NIATx process, they need reassurance that this is different. Make sure that change projects are pilot tests and make sure each change cycle is brief and an incremental change. Share data with staff. They need to know if what they are doing is working and if it isn't, then remember that abandoning a change is one of the three options.

If staff are resistant because they don't understand why change is necessary or are skeptical that the process can be improved, take the time to explain the project thoroughly and get them involved. Ask for their input for ideas to test. Get feedback from them about proposed changes. Make sure to keep them updated as to the progress of the project, and share with them any graphs or charts that demonstrate improvement. Have the resistant staff do the walk-through with another person who's completely ignorant of the process. It may help them to see the process with new eyes.

Above all, listen to their concerns and make sure that they know you understand those concerns and are taking them into account as you move forward with the project.

3. The Problem: Infrequent Feedback from Data

Team members may become frustrated if they aren't seeing evidence of progress on a regular basis.

Possible Symptoms: Diminishing enthusiasm; team seems lost

The Fix: Don't wait until the end of a change project to analyze data. Develop quick, simple methods for capturing data on a weekly basis—even if it means scribbling in a notebook—and review the data with the team. Consider intermediate measures that could be tracked to make sure that a change is being implemented correctly. For instance, if you are trying to reduce wait times by freeing up clinicians from nonclinical tasks, you might track the amount of time that clinicians are spending on paperwork to see if it decreases.

4. The Problem: Diminishing Enthusiasm
A project starts off full-steam ahead, only to flounder later as the team begins to lose interest, energy, and motivation.

Possible Causes: Infrequent feedback from data; ineffectual change leader, team seems lost; achievements feel minor or insignificant; the project is unmanageable; lack of communications and meetings; tasks have been assigned to the wrong people.

Possible Symptoms: Team is not generating ideas; project is dragging on

The Fix: Waning enthusiasm may be a symptom of an underlying problem that should be addressed. Begin by considering reasons why enthusiasm might be faltering, taking into account the other common barriers discussed in this section.

Even if a project is running smoothly, it's not unusual for excitement to wear down a bit as time goes on. If this is the case, it's up to the change leader and executive sponsor to keep momentum going and keep the team motivated:

- Re-engage the team by challenging them to come up with new ideas.
- Make sure the team is aware of the progress that has been made.
- Remind them regularly that their efforts are truly making a difference and improving the organization.
- Celebrate when goals are achieved, even if they are minor.
- Consider that maybe you have gone as far as you can with this particular aim and put together a different team to work on a different issue.

5. The Problem: Insufficient Time for Testing
When change team members are already overburdened by their duties outside of the change effort, they may not be able to devote the necessary time and effort to pilot testing changes, which can result in delays or ineffective tests.

Possible Causes: Tasks have been assigned to the wrong people

Possible Symptoms: Inaccurate or incomplete data; project is dragging on

The Fix: Head off the problem before it starts by taking a team member's normal workload into account when assigning tasks, and discuss with the team member how he will be able to fulfill the additional responsibilities. If the problem is already occurring, talk with the team member about his schedule to find ways to free up time. If necessary, confer with the executive sponsor to discuss how the team member's current assignments could be reallocated to free up his time for the change effort. Identify changes that produce more time for staff.

6. The Problem: Customers Don't Notice Improvement

Increasing customer satisfaction and responding to customer needs should be a priority of any change project. If the improvements you are making are going unnoticed by clients, and are not enhancing their experience of your services, it may be a sign that you haven't adequately addressed their needs.

Possible Causes: Choosing the wrong problem, solutions that don't address the measure

Possible Symptoms: Staff resistance, not much change in data measures

The Fix: Return to the first principle of NIATx, and reexamine your project from the customer's point of view. Consider performing another walk-through, and use any means at your disposal—such as surveys or focus groups—to get customer feedback and use that feedback to shape the improvement effort.

7. The Problem: Inaccurate or Incomplete Data

126

Data that are inaccurately recorded, incompletely recorded, or not relevant to the aim at hand can derail a change effort and act as a barrier to progress.

Possible Causes: Tasks have been assigned to the wrong people; insufficient time for testing; team members are not being held accountable

Possible Symptoms: Team seems lost; no improvement on measures, missing data

The Fix: Review the data collection tips in Chapter 7 and perform a walk-through of your current data collection methods. Is the process as simple and easy as possible? Could it be simplified? Take care to:

- Review the instructions you developed for the data collection method to make sure they are clear and unambiguous.

- Make sure that you are collecting the relevant data by creating a flowchart to demonstrate exactly how the data are connected to your aim.

- Ask to observe the team member serving as data-collector as he does a walk-through of the collecting process to determine where and why mistakes are being made, and explain to the data-collector if something is being done wrong, and the correct way of doing it.

- If necessary, re-assign data collection responsibilities to a different team member.

- The most common issue with data is that people measure the wrong thing, and so the change project doesn't seem to move the measure. Reassess whether the changes being made really relate to the measure being used.

8. The Problem: Team Seems Lost or Is Drifting From Goal

The team is losing focus and seems unsure of what they are meant to be accomplishing. Or, they are getting off track and are drifting away from the aim of the change project.

Possible Causes: The project is unmanageable; ineffectual change leader; inaccurate or incomplete data; lack of communication and meetings; infrequent feedback from data

Possible Symptoms: Diminishing enthusiasm; project is dragging on; team is not generating ideas

The Fix:

- Check in with team members regularly to ask what they are working on, and how it directly relates to the goal.

- Keep meetings focused and brief by creating an agenda in advance, and stick to that agenda.

- When making decisions about what to do next, clearly explain to members why you are doing it, and how it relates to the goal.

- Consider whether your project might be unmanageable and should be broken up into multiple projects (see below).

9. The Problem: Team Members are Not Being Held Accountable

A change project's success depends on the full participation and effort of everyone on the change team, as well as other staff involved in testing changes. If anyone is not fulfilling her responsibilities thoroughly or efficiently enough, it can throw the whole project off balance, or create undue burden on the other team members who are forced to pick up the slack.

Possible Causes: Ineffectual change leader

Possible Symptoms: Inaccurate or incomplete data; project is dragging on

The Fix:

- Clearly communicate what's expected of each member of the team, and make it clear that everyone will be held accountable.

- When assigning tasks, explain when you need the task to be accomplished, or let the team member set her own deadline by asking how long she thinks it will take.

- Keep track of the deadlines that you or the team member have set, and be sure to follow up to make sure that the deadlines are met.

10. The Problem: Achievements Feel Minor or Insignificant

Frustration can build when the outcomes of a change project seem disproportionately small compared to the time and effort put into it, or if progress toward the goal is happening in small increments.

Possible Causes: Project is unmanageable; not addressing key problems

Possible Symptoms: Diminishing enthusiasm; infrequent feedback from data

The Fix: Significant improvement cannot always be achieved through one large change; often it requires a number of smaller changes that add up to a big improvement. Talk with the team about this to help them understand that the effort is not futile, and make sure you focus your attention on a single aim and perform as many rapid-change cycles as necessary.

11. The Problem: The Project Is Unmanageable

It's not uncommon, particularly on the first change project, for a team to bite off more than it can chew, leading to a project that is undefined, overwhelming, unmanageable, and essentially untenable.

Possible Causes: Lack of understanding of PDSA process

Possible Symptoms: Diminishing enthusiasm; inaccurate or incomplete data; team seems lost; project is dragging on; achievements feel minor or insignificant

The Fix: Rein the project in.

- Examine the project to see how it could be broken up into chunks, and prioritize which one should be focused on first.

- Start small by holding off on tackling difficult projects until you have some process improvement experience under your belt. Work with the team to figure out what could be tested in the next few days, and do just that step.

- Bear in mind that the first change project is as much about learning about process improvement and getting better at it as it is about making the improvement. Use the opportunity to build a foundation of knowledge on which to base further projects.

12. The Problem: Change Leader Doesn't Feel Empowered to Make Decisions

Change projects can stall if the change leader doesn't feel that she has the authority to make decisions quickly.

Possible Causes: Poor direction from executive sponsor, wrong choice for change leader

Possible Symptoms: Project is dragging on; nothing is getting accomplished

The Fix:

- Confer with the change leader to establish parameters for the limits to her authority, granting as much leeway as is feasible.

- Empower the change leader by encouraging her to take charge and feel confident in her decisions.

- The change leader should pass this empowerment on to the change team, encouraging them to develop and test their own ideas for change.

13. The Problem: The Team isn't Generating Ideas

Change efforts rely on creative thinking to generate innovative ideas to test. If the team is failing to produce those ideas, it's difficult to make progress.

Possible Causes: Ineffectual change leader; team seems lost; diminishing enthusiasm

Possible Symptoms: Project is dragging on

The Fix:

- Use the tips discussed in chapter 4, such as Nominal Group Technique, in brainstorming sessions.

- Create an atmosphere of encouragement by stressing to the team that no idea is too outlandish or off-the-wall to be brought to the floor.

- Emphasize the experimental nature of the change project.

- Encourage team members to draw on their own experiences to come up with ideas for improvement.

129

14. The Problem: Lack of Communication and Meetings

During a change project, it's important to make sure that everyone involved is on the same page, has up-to-date information, and works together to decide what happens next. If the team has difficulty finding time to meet, the project may be delayed.

Possible Causes: Ineffectual change leader

Possible Symptoms: Team is lost; diminishing enthusiasm; project is dragging on

The Fix: Although it can be difficult to find time for the whole change team to meet, it's important to find ways to communicate frequently and regularly. It can be as simple as gathering everyone together for a few minutes in the hallway to quickly review progress and discuss what to do next. Any meeting, no matter how brief or informal, is better than no meeting at all; don't put off meeting until everyone on the team can agree on a time to sit down for two hours in a conference room. Sneak in meetings when you can so the project can keep moving forward without delays.

15. The Problem: Ineffectual Change Leader

In Chapter 4, we discussed the skills and qualities required of a good change leader. If the change project is not progressing as you had hoped, one possibility is that the change leader you've chosen isn't right for the job. The change leader must organize the effort, engage the team, and engender creative thinking. If any of these characteristics are lacking, it's easy for the project to go off the rails.

Possible Causes: Poor selection by executive sponsor change leader not given clear direction, change leader not given adequate time or authority

Possible Symptoms: Project is dragging on; diminishing enthusiasm; team is lost; team members aren't held accountable; team isn't generating ideas; lack of communications and meetings; tasks have been assigned to the wrong people

The Fix: If it seems the change leader has the essential qualities of a leader but isn't applying them to the project, try meeting with him to explain what's expected and what needs to change. If, on the other hand, the situation seems hopeless, bring the current change project to a close and begin a new one with a different leader.

16. The Problem: Tasks Have Been Assigned to the Wrong People

There will be bumps in the road if a team member or staffer has been assigned tasks that are unsuitable for her capabilities.

Possible Causes: Wrong change leader, poor selection of team members, unclear direction from executive sponsor.

Possible Symptoms: The project makes no progress.

The Fix:

- When assigning a task, rather than choosing the first person who volunteers, make an effort to match the task with the person who has the required skill set, and has enough time to be thorough.

- Reassign tasks as needed.

- If necessary, disband the team and create a new team more appropriate for the endeavor.

In Summary

Think of these common barriers—or others that you encounter—as opportunities for rapid-cycle testing. By making adjustments and testing them for short periods of time, you'll learn a lot about your organization and make progress toward removing barriers to change.

Chapter 11: Sustainability

What Is Sustainability?

O nce you've used the NIATx model to identify and test a process improvement change that successfully addresses your chosen aim, you may be tempted to think the hard part is over. In some ways, though, the work has just begun. In the final phase of a change project, which we call the sustainability phase, you need to focus on successfully maintaining the change, and the improved outcomes that it's meant to create.

What do we mean by "sustainability"? For our purposes, sustainability means being able to stick with the new way of doing things and keep getting that improved outcome that prompted you to make the change in the first place. Sustainability means maintaining the gain in the long term, not reverting to the old methods (and thus, the old, unsatisfactory outcomes).

When a change is successfully sustained, it means that the new method or procedure has become fully integrated into the existing system and culture of your organization. Furthermore, the new methods are stable enough to withstand and even take advantage of other organizational changes you may make in the future, and is flexible enough to adapt to unexpected circumstances or events. Because our model is based on the idea of continuous improvement, sustaining a change means not reverting to the old way of doing things, but always thinking of ways to improve the new procedure even more. The new process should be evolving and never regressing.

It's easy to fall into the trap of thinking that your change will sustain itself with little or no effort on your part, or that you'll be able to deal with threats and problems as they come up. According to the British National Health Service, over 70 percent of change efforts fail to be sustained beyond the first six months. To avoid this fate, you'll need to put serious thought and effort into creating and implementing a plan for sustainability, and following through on it.

Although the sustainability phase technically begins once a new process has been implemented, you should be developing a plan for sustainability as early as possible. Ideally, you should be thinking about it from the very beginning of a change project, before any ideas have even been tested.

Keeping sustainability in mind from the beginning of the project is beneficial because it allows you to evaluate changes tested in PDSA Cycles not only by whether they yielded improvement in the data, but also whether they'll be sustainable in the long term. In essence, the potential for sustainability will be one of the guiding factors in the pilot testing process. As you'll see when you encounter our sustainability model, the model helps you evaluate a new process against a number of factors that predict whether the change is likely to be

131

sustained. Using the model early, before deciding which changes to implement, allows you to shape those changes so that they better align with factors that favor long-term sustainability.

Furthermore, you'll be able to use what you've learned about sustainability to shape future improvement projects, designing them with sustainability in mind from the get-go.

In this section, we guide you through the sustainability phase by introducing you to the Sustainability Model. The model, developed by the British National Health Service in collaboration with our team here at the University of Wisconsin–Madison, is a self-assessment tool that relies on 10 key factors to identify and address the strengths and weaknesses of a given change project, and it will help predict the likelihood that you will be able to sustain the change.

Getting Started

You've already used the NIATx model to identify and implement a process change that addresses your chosen aim, by selecting a change leader and team and using rapid-cycle testing. Here are some guidelines for actions to take as you enter the sustainability phase:

Choose a Sustain Leader: The sustain leader should be someone familiar with the change and the reasoning behind it. He should be someone who already has oversight responsibility for the processes affected by the change. The sustain leader will be responsible both for making sure that the new procedure is being followed correctly and thoroughly, and for monitoring the outcome to make sure that the improvement is not slipping. Because monitoring the data is the most active part of the sustain leader's job, it's best to select someone who would naturally be responsible for paying attention to that particular data element. Note that the sustain leader does not have to be the same person who led the change team during the project.

Codify the Change: Update process and procedures manuals to include the changed process, including the position responsible for monitoring the data in the future. Bear in mind that the procedures you're establishing should themselves be simple enough that they won't require too much training or instruction. Documentation describing the new process should thus be short and simple. If you find that clearly explaining the new procedures requires a whole book, that may be a sign the procedures are too complicated and will be difficult to sustain.

Collect and Review Data: Decide on a method of collecting and analyzing data relevant to your process change. During the sustainability phase, it's important to keep measuring data so that if improvement starts to slip, you'll know as soon as possible and will be able to identify and address the problem quickly. Keep your collection methods quick and simple, and be sure not to collect any unnecessary data. Decide which measure is important, and focus your energy on that data.

Determine What's Acceptable, and What Isn't: As you collect and compare data, you may see a certain degree of fluctuation. This is normal, and doesn't necessarily indicate a problem. Before you start, decide how much fluctuation is acceptable, and determine at what point action will be taken. As you break in the new process, revisit the parameters you've set and adjust them if necessary based on how the change is going.

Set the Date: Instead of phasing in a change, set an official start date and make sure that all details and instructions for the new procedure are clearly communicated to the appropriate staff prior to the date.

The Sustainability Model

In this section, you are introduced to the Sustainability Model, a self-assessment tool that will help you evaluate your project's strengths, weaknesses, and chances for success. Using 10 key factors, the model predicts the likelihood that your organization will be able to sustain a given change and, in doing so, allows you to craft a more sustainable change. Because the model can help in planning a successful project, it's ideal to use it for the first time at the beginning of a change project. You'll want to use it to assess and re-assess the change when it's implemented, at months 1, 3, 6, and 12, and thereafter as needed.

An Introduction to the Sustainability Model

To create the Sustainability Model, the British National Health Service, in collaboration with the University of Wisconsin–Madison, identified 10 key factors, organized around three categories, that come into play when determining a project's sustainability. These factors are:

Process:

- **Monitoring Progress:** As discussed earlier, data monitoring doesn't end with the initial test period. The success of a change effort depends on whether the organization has created a system that tracks the data during the sustain phase and is able to react quickly should the improved outcome begin to slip into unacceptable territory.

- **Adaptability:** A plan's adaptability reflects how easily the new procedure can be molded to fit cleanly into the structure of the organization, and whether it's flexible enough to be adapted to meet future needs or unexpected circumstances. An adaptable procedure is one that can withstand future organizational changes without falling apart and which can itself evolve to produce even better outcomes.

Outcome of Study

- **Credibility of Evidence:** Whether the change produces obvious, demonstrable benefits that are recognized by and clearly communicated to all people involved, and whether these benefits are supported by evidence.

- **Benefits Beyond the Patient:** An organization has a greater chance for success if staff see the change as making their own work easier or more efficient, or if it generally helps things run more smoothly. Conversely, if staff see a change as making their work lives more difficult, they will likely have a more negative attitude toward it.

Staff:

- **Training and Involvement:** In a successful sustain effort, staff members at all levels are engaged in the change process from the beginning, are encouraged to offer their own input, are adequately trained in the new policies or procedures, and are kept up-to-date on progress and developments.

- **Attitudes:** Staff members are on board with the change and feel empowered by it. They understand why the change is necessary and how it will be beneficial. They believe that the change can be sustained.

- **Senior Leaders:** The degree to which the organization's senior leaders take responsibility for the sustain effort and are willing to put the necessary time and effort into it.

- **Clinical Leaders:** The degree to which the organization's clinical leaders take responsibility for the sustain effort and are willing to put the necessary time and effort into it.

Organization:

- **Infrastructure:** This factor refers to whether the organization has sufficient facilities, equipment, and staff to sustain the change; whether policies and job descriptions are clearly defined and communicated; and whether there are good lines of communication in place.

- **Fit with Goals and Culture:** This factor relates to how easily the change will fit into the existing structure and culture of the organization. It also relates to whether change is in sync with the organization's values and mission, as well as whether the organization has a history of successful change efforts and how accepting of change the organization is in general.

The sustainability model offers a structured format for your organization to evaluate a change project based on these 10 factors.

———————

The Sustainability Model has been tested for accuracy on over 200 change projects.

Who should use the sustainability model? To get a full range of viewpoints, we recommend that multiple staff members individually complete the model; afterward, the team can discuss and analyze their results.

To use the online version of the Sustainability Model, visit the Process Improvement Toolbox at www.niatx.net.

135

Examples of Sustainability from Four NIATx Agencies

Gateway to Prevention and Recovery, Norman, Oklahoma

Change Implemented	Improvements/ Gains	Sustainability Duration	Sustainability Tips
To reduce wait time to assessments *Gateway to Prevention and Recovery:* • Made appointments no more than five working days from first contact; eliminated unnecessary paperwork, shifting some information collection from clinical staff to support staff • Used computer-based self-assessments • Double-booked assessments • Offered walk-ins four days per week	By December 2005, virtually all assessments were walk-ins (0 days to assessment). Consequently, no-shows to assessment dropped to 0%. Days to treatment were reduced from over 80 days in November 2004 to less than a week in August 2006.	Despite changes in the clinic's workforce, the project began its sustain period in December 2005, one year following implementation of the change project.	Have listening sessions with consumers to clear up false assumptions about consumer needs.
Baseline data for Nov–Dec 2004 was 14 days to assessment; no-show rate 37%.			

PORT Human Services, Greenville North Carolina

Change Implemented	Improvements/ Gains	Sustainability Duration	Sustainability Tips
To reduce no-shows to admissions *PORT Human Services:* • Implemented reminder phone calls and letters • Increased physician availability • Provided same-day physician appointments and dosing Baseline data for no-shows was 20% and admissions were 107 in 2004.	After implementing changes, no-shows decreased to 11%. Admissions increased to 178 in 2005 (a 60% increase). As of July 2006, physician availability decreased due to the increased demand for services.	PORT Human Services implemented the project in April 2004, and the project began its sustain period by the end of that year.	It's critical that program managers and supervisors understand the importance of sustainability. Management must understand that fostering sustainability and spread is an important part of their role in a treatment agency.

PROTOTYPES, California

Change Implemented	Improvements/ Gains	Sustainability Duration	Sustainability Tips
To reduce no-shows to intake *PROTOTYPES:* • Implemented motivational interviewing with outpatient clients during clinical assessment. • Baseline, pre-change data showed a three-month average rate (Oct–Dec 2004) of 36% for intake no-shows.	Following implementation of motivational interviewing during clinical assessment, no-shows to intake dropped to an annual average of 10.08% (Jan–Dec 2005). From Jan–June 2006, the gains observed because of this change project continued to increase, with an average no-show rate of 2.45%.	Eight months after beginning the change project (August 2005), the change team shifted to sustaining the gains it had generated.	Keep actively pursuing continuation of change behavior with staff. Continue daily, weekly, and monthly measures to ensure changes are being implemented and gains are continuing. Make sure all staff involved in the project are properly trained. At *PROTOTYPES*, additional staff members are cross-trained to perform assessments, so the change team ensured these extra staff members were trained in motivational interviewing techniques

Southwest Florida Addiction Services, Fort Myers, Florida

Change Implemented	Improvements/ Gains	Sustainability Duration	Sustainability Tips
To reduce no-shows to assessment *Southwest Florida Addiction Services (SWFAS):* • Required clinicians to meet a productivity goal of 20 hours of direct service per week. The change leader monitored clinician productivity and provided feedback to clinicians. • Implemented walk-in appointments for self-referrals and clients referred by the Department of Children and Families (DCF). For the 12 months prior to the change project, the average number of assessments per month was 112. The no-show rate for court-related services clients was 60%; staff completed four assessments for self- and DCF-referred clients per week.	The average number of direct service hours rose by 13.5% from February to April 2005. The average number of assessments rose from 112 to 122 per month. Wait time to assessment decreased from five weeks to less than 1 week (Dec 2004–June 2005) No-show rate for assessments decreased from 60% to 44%. Assessments for DCF and self-referred clients doubled from an average of four to an average of eight per week. Time to assessment equaled 4.7 calendar days. .	By Oct 2005, 9 months after the change project began, SWFAS shifted to sustaining the gains. Holidays and staff vacations, as well as hurricane season, affected some of the measures, but the change team has been discussing solutions to this problem.	Designate one person to track a specific measure, such as time until the next available appointment. Keep measurement simple. Measures that require a lot of time to track don't result in timely feedback. Have a team set a target and let everyone on staff know. Give regular feedback on your measures to all staff in the department, celebrating when the target is met, and prompting action when it's not. Provide regular feedback to the executive sponsor. He can provide congratulations or support when necessary.

In Summary

The Sustainability Model was designed to be used on one specific change project at a time. It isn't meant to be used on multiple projects at once, or as an assessment tool to predict whether an organization will generally be successful in sustaining change efforts. Using the Model can help you not only choose improvement projects that have the best chances of being sustained, but also help you see how chances of success change as a project moves forward.

Chapter 12: Spread

Though NIATx change projects typically address one of the identified aims, all change projects should have a separate, broader objective: increasing the organization's capacity for improvement. NIATx organizations do not simply carry out one change project and leave it at that. The idea is to build process improvement into the structure of the agency, getting better at it with each subsequent project, and spreading positive innovations throughout the organization.

In this chapter, we examine the notion of spread: the diffusion of improved processes throughout the organization. NIATx change projects are intentionally limited in scope to one aim + one location + one population. There are a number of reasons that we have set these limits in place, including simplifying the project, making it more manageable, and enabling more meaningful data collection. However, after you've determined you have a successful, sustainable change and your project is complete, you can begin to explore ways to share your innovative new process with other departments or service areas within your organization.

Taking an active, strategic approach to spreading innovation ensures that no knowledge or experience will go to waste. The lessons learned and skills developed during a successful change project should be strategically spread throughout the organization. If, on the contrary, the knowledge gained during a project is not used for further improvement efforts, it means that the potential benefits of the project have not been fully realized, and an opportunity has been lost.

Spreading innovation is not simply a matter of replicating the same new process that was successful in one context and implementing it in a different location. In fact, the apparent simplicity of spread can be deceptive, which is why we stress that it's important to come up with a strategy for spreading innovation. Don't think that just because a new process worked successfully in one area of your organization that it will succeed, without modification, in other areas. In fact, much of the original work involved with crafting the new process— examination of customer needs, data collection, refinement through testing—will need to be repeated in the spread project.

What Works, What Doesn't

According to NIATx members, a successful spread project:

- Identifies weaknesses and processes to correct a key problem

- Is simple to implement

- Gives quick results

- Reduces workload

- Can be quantified

- Is a team effort

- Is a small, simple change idea

Whereas an unsuccessful spread project:

- Attempts to implement a change not important to your customer

- Lacks investigation into the root cause of the problem before implementation

- Is hard to implement

- Gives results months rather than days or weeks after implementation

- Does not improve staff workload

- Is driven by research protocols

- Lacks staff buy-in

- Is too large in scope with not enough resources

142

Choosing Which Innovations to Spread

The first step in spreading innovation is deciding which changes seem suitable for other parts of your organization. Not every change can necessarily be seen as a candidate for spread. Candidates for spread should be process changes that have been both implemented and sustained successfully, to positive effect, and which have not only produced improved outcomes but have met an enthusiastic reception from staff and customers, essentially generating enthusiasm for the concept of process improvement.

Professionals from within the NIATx network have identified five attributes of a successful change, based on their own experiences. Use them to help evaluate which changes should be candidates for spread:

- A positive effect on financial sustainability
- Data that show a positive impact
- Simple, tangible change that has been sustained in the organization
- Positive consumer feedback
- Strong staff interest

Choosing Where to Spread

Similarly, not every innovation will be suited to every area where it could theoretically be applied. When spreading an innovation, strategize by defining the spread project much like you defined the original change project: one location and one population. When deciding these factors, it's important to consider:

- How is the new location different from the original location?
- What new barriers might you encounter at the new location?
- Why is the change necessary at the new location? Will it be an improvement there?
- Who are the customers at the new location, how are their needs different from those of the original location?

Anticipate Barriers

It's key to use the knowledge you gained during the original change project to your advantage when spreading a change. What problems did you encounter? Will those problems interfere with the new project, and how might they be avoided? When and why did staff come on board with the original project? Examine the factors that might have created resistance and the factors that helped overcome that resistance.

In a larger sense, think about what you've learned, not just about process improvement, but about your organization and its strengths and weaknesses. Change projects serve as opportunities to identify what your organization does well, and where it tends to falter. This information will help you play to those strengths, and avoid those weaknesses, as you attempt to spread innovation.

143

Re-Examine the Needs of the Customer

The first NIATx principle is no less essential here than in any change project: Understand the needs of the customer before you attempt to implement change. Don't assume that the customers at the new location have the same needs as those at the original location. Once again, the most effective tool for achieving the kind of understanding is the walk-through. By walking through the way things are done in the location you'll be working with, you'll be more aware of the differences and similarities in terms of customer needs.

Adapt the Process as Necessary

During a change project, ideas that have worked successfully for other agencies are adapted to fit the circumstances of your organization. The same idea goes when spreading an improvement idea to a different area of your organization: Be open and enthusiastic about adapting it to fit seamlessly into this new context. Look at the new site on its own terms, without assuming that conditions are the same, or that client needs are the same.

How are the needs of the customer different at this location/area? How should that affect the shaping of the new process?

Does the innovation need to be adapted for the new context and, if so, how? Think about the ways in which the new location differs in terms of infrastructure, policies, staffing structure, customer needs, and attitudes—different departments often have different outlooks and cultures. Is the hierarchy of authority more rigid? More egalitarian? Do staff there feel emboldened to share their opinions and participate in the steering of policy? Characterizing the new environment will help you identify ways the process should be tweaked and will also help you determine the best way approach to take with staff.

Strategizing Communications

Clear, thorough communication is essential to successful spread. You must be able to communicate the innovation to key players in the arena to which you are attempting to spread the process. This means both explaining how the process works, and why it's an improvement on the old way of doing things.

How does knowledge get transferred from person to person in an organization? An essential part of spreading improvement is ensuring that the knowledge gleaned during an improvement project is not limited to the sphere of people who worked directly on that project—knowledge should be communicated throughout the agency.

One way to figure out the best means of communicating ideas is to consider your own experiences in apprehending ideas from within the organization. What was the most effective means of communication? Take time to consider the best methods of communication, basing your evaluation on your own experiences with your organization. Think about a time when you learned of a new idea or policy from another part of the organization. How was it communicated to you? Was that communication effective? Was its argument convincing?

Facilitate Observation

Another facet of communication when spreading a change is making staff in the new location aware of how the process works and how it benefits customers and the organization. The best way to do this isn't to tell them, it's to show them: Invite employees from the new location to a demonstration of how the process works at the original location. Showing them how well the process has worked in the original location—how it better serves clients, makes work more efficient, produces better outcomes—can help them understand how the new process operates and reduce skepticism and resistance.

Test and Track Outcomes

Again, it's important not to blindly assume that a change that was successful in another arena will (a) work on a practical level and (b) produce improved outcomes when you attempt to spread it to a new location. For that reason, you should refine the process through testing and measure outcomes to determine whether it yields improvement in the new location. Adapt and test the change just as you did when originally crafting it, and keep an open mind to the ways in which it might need to change.

146

Chapter 13: Learning Collaboratives

A gencies benefit from learning from each other and getting support from others making similar changes to their programs. Agencies attempting a change project are strongly encouraged to network with other NIATx agencies, share ideas, offer support, and learn from one another. One way this happens is through a learning collaborative.

The Benefits of a Learning Collaborative

Setting up a learning collaborative is a systematic and effective way to facilitate this kind of interagency networking and to foster constructive relationships on a system level between the payer/purchaser of treatment services (such as the state, a managed care company, or other payer or regulator) and the treatment providers (the treatment agencies) within the system. In a learning collaborative, someone convenes organizations to launch their own synchronized change projects. A single agency could create a learning collaborative from multiple units or departments that are working on change projects. A payer could develop a learning collaborative with organizations that it funds. A trade association could convene a learning collaborative with its members or a small group of its members interested in improving a specific aspect of their work. The group process of learning together and sharing success and struggles fits with how adults learn and enables continued progress of the effort and sustains the changes made. It's helpful to have a NIATx coach or experienced change leader to facilitate the collaborative process.

Learning collaboratives are beneficial for both providers and purchasers for a number of reasons:

- **Training and Guidance:** Agencies participating in a learning collaborative receive organized training in process improvement from someone with experience—either a coach or someone who has already used this method to do process improvement.

- **Structure:** Change projects can be difficult, especially for first-timers. It's easy for projects to meander or stall, or for the team to become frustrated or confused about how to proceed. Learning collaboratives impose a structure onto the improvement process that establishes expectations, guidelines and time frames. This structure helps participants plan out their projects and stay focused on making progress.

- **Peer Support:** One of the points that we like to stress to an organization initiating a process improvement project is that it is not alone. There will likely be times during the project when the team will get stuck, at a loss for ideas, unsure how to proceed, or confused as to why progress isn't being made. If the project is being conducted in isolation, these frustrations can be deadly to the project. Learning collaboratives can overcome these barriers because they offer participating agencies an opportunity to discuss challenges with other agencies going through the same thing, sharing ideas and getting feedback. Organizations in a learning collaborative will learn from each others' successes and mistakes, creating a supportive atmosphere in which everyone is working together toward the same goal.

- **Relationships:** In a learning collaborative, treatment organizations develop relationships with each other, and with the sponsoring organization. The positive, constructive interaction that occurs during a learning collective can alleviate the tension often found in the payer–provider relationship. Rather than believing themselves to be on opposite sides of the fence, the payer and provider organizations discover through learning collaboratives that they are on the same side, that they want the same things, and that what is good for one is good for both. In addition, providers that at one level are competitors can find common ground and work constructively to improve the entire system of care.

- **System-wide Improvement:** Learning collaboratives yield improvement on an individual level for the participating providers, but also on a system wide level. The collective effort put into a learning collaborative means the entire system is being improved to work more efficiently and deliver better care. By opening up channels of communication between payer and provider, learning collaboratives also allow the opportunity for the payer to solicit ideas from providers as to how the system could be improved to increase access and retention.

- **Experience:** Learning collaboratives not only produce successful change projects; they also produce a group of organizations that are knowledgeable about and experienced in process improvement, and who can serve as mentors and guides for other organizations within the system, helping to spread the culture of improvement.

The System-level Change Project:
When learning collaboratives are part of a system-wide effort to improve service delivery, they should include a change project at the system level not unlike the provider-oriented change projects that we describe in this book. At the system level, the payer/regulator looks for innovations and process changes that will improve a targeted aim, using input and feedback from the providers participating in the learning collaborative, as well as a walk-through, to develop changes to test. For example, when Maine's Office of Substance Abuse conducted a system-level change project that involved faxing authorization paperwork to providers (rather than mailing it, as had been done in the past), no-show rates dropped by 28 percent.

Setting Up a Learning Collaborative

The convener of a learning collaborative should be the highest executive authority of the purchasing organization, a regulatory body or of a large multi-site organization. This guide is therefore aimed at the leadership of a system-wide change project, although this may be useful for providers who wish to acquaint themselves with the learning collaborative process.

Getting Started

1. Identify a Project Coordinator

- Coordinate meetings, including: Arranging a convenient date and location; booking an appropriate venue, and ensuring that the site is set up appropriately (so people can work in groups but still see the trainer, for example); setting up a registration system for participants; preparing handouts for participants; planning meeting agendas and articulating desired goals and objectives; helping prepare content for the meeting; preparing a post-meeting summary to distribute to participants and to those who were unable to attend.

- Facilitate communications, including: Providing information and updates about the collaborative to both internal and external stakeholders; creating and using a system of communication to share updates, announcements, meeting minutes, agendas, paperwork, and other relevant information to project stakeholders; answering questions from participating providers; and following up when a provider misses a meeting.

- Coordinate site visits (if they are to be held) to participating providers or sites, including: scheduling visits; preparing materials to be brought to the site (such as NIATx resources); preparing an agenda prior to the visit; and a detailed summary after the visit.

- Arrange teleconferences, including: Determining convenient dates and times; communicating logistics and agendas with participants; preparing a post-teleconference phone call summary to distribute.

- Track progress, including: Developing a system to track progress both for individual providers and across all providers (aggregate progress); preparing progress summary reports to be distributed in meetings; helping providers as necessary with data collection/progress tracking.

2. Visit niatx.net to view the many tools and resources available to assist in convening a learning collaborative.

3. Select participants to invite to join the collaborative

How will people be invited to participate? What are the criteria for participation? Do they need an introduction of some sort to develop interest and enthusiasm?

The selection and invitation process can be key to the success of the learning collaborative process. Just like inviting people to participate in change teams, inviting people to participate in a learning collaborative is a process of engagement. They need to understand that they are

149

working on process improvement and not that they are bad managers or have bad programs, but that they are being provided with an opportunity to improve on the good work they already do. In our most successful learning collaborative, providers have been asked to apply or to complete a walk-through prior to participation so they can come to the first training with an open mind and an eye to seeing their organization the way the client sees it.

4. Hold an introduction meeting

Once potential participants have been selected, the system-level executive sponsor or the project coordinator should invite the senior management of the selected agencies or divisions/departments to an introductory meeting, which can be held in person or by teleconference, if necessary. During this meeting, the following information should be shared:

- Explain the purpose of the learning collaborative, the concept behind process improvement, and the kinds of challenges these projects often face.
- Provide details as to the process and timeframe of the collaborative.
- Explain what will be required of the participating agencies.
- Arrange for the change leader of a successful change project to do a presentation on his or her agency's experience, and the ways that the agency benefited from the project.

Leading the Collaborative

There is a good degree of flexibility when it comes to the structure of the learning collaborative; the following guidelines reflect a structural model that has proven effective for past NIATx collaboratives.

Month 1: Kickoff Workshop

At the start of the project, organize a one- or two-day workshop to be facilitated by someone experienced, possibly a NIATx coach or someone who has participated in a NIATx learning collaborative already. This workshop will kick off the providers' change projects, offering information about the NIATx model as well as encouragement and motivation.

It's key to remember that the kickoff meeting and subsequent meetings should be interactive; participants must have the opportunity to discuss their experiences, ask questions, and network with each other.

Meeting Objectives:

- Build enthusiasm for process improvement.
- Explain process improvement from a procedural standpoint, including how to run pilot tests.
- Create a project charter for beginning a change project.

- Go over the timeline for the collaborative as it relates to each agency's project.

- Present case studies of successful NIATx change projects.

- Discuss promising practices, including strategies for understanding client needs.

- Allow the opportunity for prioritization of needs based on each agency's walk-through and data findings.

- Stage multiple interactive sessions to discuss process improvement strategies and tips for avoiding or overcoming common barriers.

Hold a Remote Collaborative

If holding a face-to-face meeting is impossible, there's an online training course on Process Improvement 101 available for free at www.niatx.net, or you may wish to share this book or other NIATx resources with participants. It's possible to do the entire learning collaborative remotely as long as there is someone responsible for ensuring that people follow through on their tasks prior to and in between learning collaborative calls. A face-to-face kick-off or introduction seems to work best, but sometimes budget or logistics make that impossible. Any of these recommendations can be adapted to suit the needs of your particular set of circumstances.

(151)

Months 5–11: Regular Meetings

Throughout the project, the change leaders and executive sponsors should meet at least once a month in person or via teleconference, to share experiences, offer progress reports, ask questions, and receive technical assistance. It's helpful to sometimes invite outside speakers (remember the principle of getting ideas from outside the organization). At each meeting, be sure to give each organization or department time to share its experience and progress, and leave time for the organizations to network with one another.

Month 11–12: Completion Conference

At the end of the collaborative, convene a final meeting to give participating agencies a chance to report on their progress and celebrate their successes. This meeting should also give them the opportunity to share advice and lessons learned, and to discuss ideas for sustainability.

Structure the meeting around 15-minute presentations from each participating agency about their experience and how the project went, then have an open discussion. This meeting acts as a celebration, a learning opportunity, and a bookend to the formal project. If it can be done face-to-face, that is preferred.

Local governments play an important role in improving substance abuse and mental health services. The case study that follows shows how payers and providers can work together in a local learning collaborative to improve services within a set geographic area.

Case Study: Learning Collaboratives

In the center of New York State, Onondaga County is home to about 450,000 residents and includes the city of Syracuse. In 2006, the Onondaga County Department of Mental Health (OCDMH) in New York launched a NIATx local learning collaborative to promote the use of evidence-based practices (EBPs) in its chemical dependency and mental health services programs[1].

The learning collaborative's first project was to test the use of Contingency Management (CM) to reduce no-shows and increase continuation in chemical dependency treatment programs. CM is a behavioral therapy that supports treatment goals with incentives and consequences. OCDMH recruited four of its contracted treatment organizations to participate in the project. Two of the larger organizations in this group represent more than 80% of the chemical dependency services provided in Onondaga County.

All participating organizations received training in the NIATx model of process improvement. The participants met monthly to share successes and challenges in testing CM to reduce no-shows and increase continuation. Participants also received regular support from an expert NIATx coach.

While the monthly meetings kept providers connected and motivated to continue to work on the changes, individualized coaching was critical to the collaborative's success. The NIATx coach brought other expertise and helped the collaborative participants stay focused on their aims.

The organizations began to test CM using the NIATx rapid-cycle model in late 2006 and early 2007. Changes were implemented for a single group within each organization, with an average attendance of eight to twelve people.

No-show rates over a six-month period improved for: (a) an evening out-patient group from 61% to 33.3% by serving a light meal (Soup for Group); (b) second appointments for out-patients and intensive outpatients from 49% to 13% by offering day planners to recipients; and (c) an outpatient treatment group from 30% to 9% by offering refreshments. (See chart to the right).

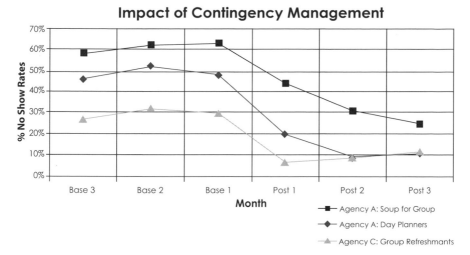

Impact of Contingency Management

Aside from obvious improvements in no-show rates, implementing Contingency Management (CM) helped cultivate an entrepreneurial spirit among participating organizations. While providers were concerned about the expense of incentives such as food, the CM projects produced a significant return on investment through increased billings.

OCDMH conducted a second learning collaborative that included six of its contracted mental health providers. This group worked on increasing continuation in treatment, among other aims.

153

The two collaboratives offered key lessons for other payers considering forming a local learning collaborative. These include:

1. Establish a clear plan and shared vision: A shared vision enhances engagement and creates the basis of the collaborative.

2. One size does not fit all: Diversity of implementation among collaborative members ensures ongoing relevance for all participants.

3. Data fuels engagement: Using the NIATx model and a data-driven approach to discuss how to adjust changes based on results supports learning and teamwork.

4. Quality over quantity: Implementing a local learning collaborative is like driving on ice: gain traction first, and then accelerate carefully.

5. Pay for participation: Providers are less likely to volunteer to participate if they feel they might lose revenue. OCDMH offered mini-grants to organizations participating in the learning collaboratives as an incentive.

In summary

In the NIATx model of process improvement, the continuous flow of ideas among peers in a learning collaborative drives successful change projects. In a NIATx learning collaborative, a group focused on improving a specific aim meets regularly for six months to a year and works together to achieve that aim.

Chapter 14: Coaching

Ideally, in the NIATx Learning Collaborative Model, agencies attempting change are equipped with an external support network that offers training, ideas, motivation, and encouragement. One feature of this model is coaching: An agency attempting a process improvement change is assigned a NIATx coach who is skilled and experienced in process improvement to offer guidance and support for the agency, helping it to plan, implement, and sustain beneficial changes.

The coach engages all key players in the change effort, including the executive sponsor, the change leader, and the change team. The coach both trains the team in the NIATx model of process improvement and offers guidance on specific change projects and advice through regular contact via phone, e-mail, and on-site visits. Coaches share the knowledge they have gleaned from their experiences with other agencies, keep the agency focused on the task at hand, and offer ideas for trouble-shooting.

The guidance provided by the coach is not limited to the change project at hand; rather, the coach teaches the agency a process improvement model that the agency will be able to apply to other initiatives. In the big picture, working with a coach on a specific change project equips the agency with a set of skills that will enable them to successfully and independently implement future organizational changes.

What the Coach Brings to the Table

The benefits of coaching go far beyond teaching an agency how the NIATx model works. Apart from training the staff in process improvement, here are some other valuable assets the coach brings to the project:[1]

- **Enthusiasm:** The coach's presence serves as a motivator for the change leader and the team, keeping them engaged and helping them get excited about the project at hand. Regular contact with the coach will help keep momentum going, and reinvigorate the team if their energy or enthusiasm flags. At some agencies, coaches have held Process Improvement workshops for all the staff involved in the processes being addressed, as opposed to only meeting with the change team. These workshops have increased agencywide support for and interest in change projects. Further, the coach can help get everyone on board by reassuring staff who may be skeptical or negative about the project.

- **A Fresh Perspective:** When an agency has always done things the same way, it can be difficult for everyone to look outside the status quo for fresh ideas and innovative solutions to organizational problems. Certain policies and procedures may be so ingrained in the agency's culture that it's difficult for staff to conceive of any other way of doing things. The coach joins the project as an outsider, with no preconceived notions about how certain things must be done. Coaches are therefore in a better position to question the status quo, and think of outside-the-box ideas and solutions to deeply entrenched problems.

- **Experience:** In addition to bringing a fresh perspective, coaches also bring the knowledge they have gained from their experiences working with other agencies and businesses. They can draw on their knowledge of what has worked for other agencies as well as what hasn't, and they can apply that knowledge to the project at hand.

- **Focus:** One potential pitfall that a team faces when beginning a change project is thinking too big. At the start of a project, when the team is filled with enthusiasm and excited to get going, they may try to undertake more than they can handle, trying to tackle too many changes at once or thinking too broadly about the scope of the project. The coach can help the team narrow the focus to define a clear, plausible goal.

- **Data Expertise:** Data collecting is one part of the process improvement model that can be challenging. A coach who is skilled at data collection and analysis can aid the team in figuring out how it will measure and collect data, and what criteria will be used to determine whether an improvement has taken place.

- **Lasting Skills:** The coach's impact on the agency is not limited to the project at hand. The coach teaches the agency the concepts of process improvement—a new skill set, a new way of thinking, and a new way of approaching problems—and in doing so, the coach empowers the agency to apply the skills they have learned to future change projects.

Coaching Techniques That Work

Certain coaching methods and practices work better than others. Here are some tips on techniques that have been shown to be helpful and effective:

Frequent and regular contact: Weekly or biweekly telephone calls with the change leader give the leader something to rely on, add structure to the project, and instill expectations in the team. During these calls, the change leader can bounce ideas off the coach and get advice. The coach can learn about specific problems the team is encountering, offer suggestions, and brainstorm with the team leader. Frequent contact is especially important in the early stages of the project, when the leader and team are still getting their bearings.

Follow-up: It's important that the coach uses the weekly phone calls with the change leader to ask specific questions about the progress of strategies and plans they had previously discussed. The coach should not simply inquire how things are generally going; he or she should engage the team leader in a detailed conversation about what specifically has been tested or accomplished and what setbacks the team has encountered.

Critical Assessment: Once the coach has been briefed on what the team has accomplished, he should critically assess the development of the project to determine whether it's progressing well or whether a new direction might be needed. Feedback should be clearly communicated to the leaders of the change project, who may be confused about how to assess progress themselves.

Provide a Macro Perspective: The coach's role is to make sure that the team has a solid understanding of how the process improvement model works in the big picture before diving into the nitty-gritty of a specific project.

On-Site Training: When coaches visit the agency to give training workshops on specific elements of process improvement, it's not only informative for the team, but it can also bolster their enthusiasm for the project.

Contact with the Change Team: Although a coach will likely work most closely with the change leader, interaction with the change team will not only motivate the team and spread process improvement skills, but will also give the coach a better idea of the culture and organization of a particular agency. This insight will allow the coach to customize and tailor his or her direction and guidance for the given set of circumstances.

Observe and Analyze the Team: The coach should get to know the strengths and weaknesses of the team as a whole through observation and analysis. By identifying team characteristics that may be hindering the progress of the project, the coach will have a better understanding of which aspects of teamwork the group needs the most help in. For example, a team may be full of ideas but fall short on executing them; once the coach recognizes this characteristic, he or she will know to concentrate on helping the team develop execution plans.

Respect the Agency: It's important that a coach bring a fresh, outside perspective while at the same time respecting the agency's culture and hierarchies. This can be a tough balance, and the coach should be sensitive to this when presenting ideas that may face opposition in the agency so as not to create resentment among employees.

Think ahead: When the change leader or team comes up with an idea, the coach should consider the potential outcomes and trouble-shoot in advance; think of the worst-case scenario, and how it can be avoided.

Look Outside the Agency for Ideas: Coaches should consider how strategies that work for other clinics and even other types of business can be made to work for this agency, and the coach should encourage the team to do the same. It also can be helpful for the coach to talk to other coaches to get their ideas and insights.

Define His/Her Role: The coach should clearly communicate his or her role to the agency so that the change leader and team know what they can expect from the coach, and in turn what will be expected from them. The coach should make it clear that she is not there to simply "fix" the problem for the agency or tell the team exactly what to do, but rather to offer support, guidance, and ideas.

Help Define a Goal: As discussed above, an agency starting a change project may have a difficult time narrowing its focus to a clearly defined goal. The coach should help with this effort by lending his expertise to determine whether a goal is plausible within a given timeframe and helping the team create a written plan to achieve that goal.

Data-collection: The coach should help the group develop a method to collect and analyze data to track the progress of their change effort. Data collection can be challenging, and the team may need extra guidance on how to measure baseline data, and how to define what constitutes an improvement.

Teach Teamwork: Foster positive and effective collaboration by teaching Nominal Group Technique and other teamwork strategies.

Understand What's Needed at a Given Time: The coach's role is a fluid one, and changes throughout the project, as the team becomes more knowledgeable and self-reliant. The coach should be aware of this and consider what style of coaching will be the most helpful at each stage of the project. Knowing which hat to wear at a given time— cheerleader, teacher, evaluator, etc.—is the best way to ensure that the agency gets the most out of the coaching experience.

(158) **Remember the Customer:** One of the key points of the NIATx model is understanding the point of view of the customer. When helping the team brainstorm ideas, the coach should keep them focused on the customer's perspective, while the organizational perspective is kept in the background.

Methodology:

To find out which coaching techniques were the most beneficial, we conducted a study with participation from 38 substance-abuse treatment agencies across the United States, with a broad and diverse range of settings and clients. Each agency selected an executive sponsor, a change leader, and a change team to carry out a change project with the help of an assigned NIATx coach. Then, we conducted open-ended interviews with representatives from each agency (usually the change leader) about the experience, including their impressions of the coaching they had received. Each representative described his interactions with the coach and explained which practices had worked well and which hadn't. Finally, we analyzed the information and impressions that the agencies had shared with us to determine which coaching behaviors were the most useful.[2]

———

Adam Brickner, executive director of South Carolina's Phoenix Center, found coaching to be an asset when he initiated a change project focused on increasing admissions: "They gave me deadlines to target and kept me on track to report on the progress of our project."

A Case Study: Coaching

As a result of grant funding, Milwaukee County decided to redesign its addiction treatment system to be more recovery focused. "We knew that the NIATx focus on the customer and on improving systems was a good fit for our system," comments Janet Fleege, project coordinator. "We specifically wanted to work with a NIATx coach to examine the multiple handoffs between levels of care as well as from provider to provider."

Changes Implemented
Fleege and colleagues formed a change team and set about examining the processes in the system that needed improvement. Guided by NIATx coach Tom Mosgaller, "We mapped out a process flow for what a typical client experiences from intake and assessment through the assignment of a recovery support counselor, selection of a treatment approach, to discharge and follow-up." The team also developed a diagram of barriers in the process that impeded the ability to track a client six months following intake.

These activities helped the team identify early engagement as a key to a client's successful journey to recovery through the system. "We recognized that if we engage a client early in the process, we're more likely to develop a relationship that will allow tracking six months after intake." The change projects the teams began to work on focused on implementing strategies to improve the first handoff from intake to treatment.

Fleege's team then developed a set of solutions to be piloted by each agency participating in the pilot, with an emphasis on early interactions that promote engagement. "We felt that emphasis on optimizing the whole experience would result in improved relationships and the ability to track clients more successfully."

Results
The participating providers met with Fleege's team every six weeks to share progress, refine their rapid-cycle testing projects, and share next steps. At a report-out meeting the project identified the following improvements:

- An increase in the number of clients provided access or assured contact within 24 to 48 hours of first contact

- Clear plans for each client scheduled within seven days of first meeting

- Paperwork shortened to one page at initial intake

"We also feel that we have a greater focus on the client as a result of our work with NIATx," says Fleege. "Communications improved between the central intake units and the recovery support coordinators, which also helped improve hand-offs." In addition, the group noted improved collaboration between providers and recovery support coordinators.

The project has maintained a 62 percent follow-up rate and continues to work on meeting the 80 percent goal. "We have set up focus groups with recovery support coordinators to find out how we can improve, given the current process for the collection of the follow-up data," adds Fleege.

Notes

Introduction

[1]Langley, G.J., Nolan, K.M., Nolan, T.W., Norman, C. and Provost, L.,
The Improvement Guide, San Francisco: Jossey-Bass Publishers. 1996

[2]Quanbeck, Andrew R.; Madden, Lynn; Edmondson, Eldon; Ford, James H.; McConnell, K.
John; McCarty, Dennis; and Gustafson, David H. "A Business Case for Quality Improvement
in Addiction Treatment: Evidence from the NIATx Collaborative." *The Journal of Behavioral
Health Services and Research*. 1-9.

Chapter 1

[1]Swamidass, Paul E. (ed). *Encyclopedia of Production and Manufacturing*. Kluwer
Academic Publishers, 2000

[2]W. Edwards Deming, *Out of Crisis*. Boston: MIT Center for Advanced Engineering Study
Press, 1982

[3]Kenney, Charles. "The Best Practice: How the New Quality Movement is Transforming
Medicine." Public Affairs, 2008

[4]Berwick, D., Blanton Godfrey, A., and Roessner, J. *Curing Health Care: New Strategies for
Quality Improvement*. San Francisco: Jossey-Bass, 1990

Chapter 2

[1]Gustafson, D., and Schoofs Hundt, A. "Findings of Innovation Research Applied to Quality
Management Principles for Health Care." *Health Care Management Review*, 1995 20 (2)

Chapter 5

[1]Delbecq, A. Van de Ven, A., and Gustafson, D. *Group Techniques for Source Planning:
A Guide to Nominal Group and Delphi Processes*. Glenview, IL: Scott, Foresman and
Company, 1975

Chapter 6

[1]Langley, G.J., Nolan, K.M., Nolan, T.W., Norman, C. and Provost, L., *The Improvement
Guide*, San Francisco: Jossey-Bass Publishers. 1996

Chapter 13

[1]Roosa, Mathew, Scripa, Joseph S., Zastowny, Thomas R., Ford II, James H. (2011). "Using
a NIATx based local learning collaborative for performance improvement." *Evaluation and
Program Planning* 34: 390-398

Chapter 14

[1,2]"Coaching to Improve Substance Abuse Treatment Processes," Katherine J. Riley, Eldon
Edmundson, James H. Ford, II, David H. Gustafson, Dennis McCarthy. In press.

162

Glossary

Term	Definition
access	Ability to enter the treatment system
administrative practice	Processes related to office procedures that are not performed by clinical staff
admission	The point at which paperwork is completed to admit a client to treatment
agency, provider, site, organization	Used interchangeably
aim, project aim	Answers the question: What are we trying to accomplish?
aim measure	Answers the question: How will we know if a change is an improvement?
aim statement	Specific to a project and describes the aim you expect to achieve. It sometimes includes a baseline and target measure for the project. Example: Reduce no-shows to assessment appointment from 40 to 25 percent.
assessment	Determination of the need for treatment and if yes, the appropriate level of care; sometimes called evaluation.
attendance	The number of people who actually show for a group or individual session, often compared with the number that were expected
barriers	Reasons that might keep a client from attending an assessment appointment or treatment sessions
baseline measure	The data collected for the aim or cycle measure for the period of time prior to making any changes.
bottom line	The difference between revenue and expense
business case	Refers to the impact of process improvement on the organization as it relates to financial performance, staff retention/workforce development, or strategic intent. Often used to refer to the "bottom line," the difference between revenue and expense.
change cycle	Change cycle and PDSA Cycle are used interchangeably

Term	Definition
change project	Defined by one aim, one level of care, at one location, with one population. If one of these specifications changes, the executive sponsor creates and charters a new project.
change leader	Appointed by the executive sponsor to provide day-to-day leadership, energy, enthusiasm, and coordination for change projects. The change leader's work is reallocated so (s)he can dedicate adequate time to change projects. The change leader has the power and prestige to influence all levels of the organization. He/she motivates and inspires the team to fulfill the change project charter.
change project form	The change leader and team members use the change project form to document the plans for the change project and the actual changes made, along with the results.
change team	A change team is a small group of employees appointed by the executive sponsor to identify business process barriers and determine and implement rapid-cycle changes designed to improve the process.
continuation	This is a NIATx aim measured by the number of clients who attend four units of service (i.e., treatment sessions) within 30 days of their admission to treatment. The definition of a unit of service varies by level of care. For outpatient, a unit of service is a treatment session provided on a distinct date.
client, patient, customer	Addiction treatment service recipients; used interchangeably
clinical practice	Processes that relate to how clinicians or counselors provide treatment

Term	Definition
cycle measure	A measure that tells whether a change made during a particular PDSA Cycle was an improvement. The cycle measure may vary from one PDSA Cycle to the next, whereas an aim measure will remain the same for the entire change project.
engagement	A consumer's commitment to and maintenance of treatment. For NIATx purposes, engagement refers to continuation in treatment. See continuation.
evidence-based practice	An administrative or clinical practice supported by research findings and/or demonstrated application that has proven effective at improving a specific project aim.
executive sponsor	The executive sponsor is a senior leader in the organization who is passionate about improvement and who "loses sleep" over issues that need change. In the NIATx model of process improvement, the executive sponsor appoints a change leader and change team and works to remove all barriers to the change project. He/she motivates the change team through encouragement, attending team meetings periodically, monitoring the progress of the team, and acknowledging and rewarding team efforts. The executive sponsor is often the chief executive officer of the organization.
first contact/ first request for service	A client's first call or visit to request service.
flow chart	A drawing using a sequence of symbols connected by arrows. Each symbol includes a short statement about one step in a process. Flowcharts encourage an organizational focus on processes. They help identify bottlenecks, duplication, errors, and unnecessary steps; can describe a new or existing process.
intake	Collection of information to begin the assessment process
key problem	An organizational problem that the executive sponsor wants solved.

165

Term	Definition
level of care	A way to define treatment based on intensity, location, duration and assessment of a client's needs for clinical support and/or medication. In substance abuse treatment, levels of care include detoxification, residential, inpatient, outpatient, intensive outpatient, and after care or continuing care. States define these levels differently.
location	The specific place or office within an agency or site where a change project is taking place.
motivation	Readiness, willingness, and ability to change (from *Motivational Interviewing* by Miller and Rollnick)
on-demand service	Service that is available when the client requests it. Also referred to as same-day service, walk-in service.
outcome measure	The outcome measure evaluates the long-term impact of the change project for the client by assessing, for example, treatment continuation rates, employment, housing, etc.
payer	The entity paying for treatment services.
PDSA Cycle	Plan-Do-Study-Act (PDSA) Cycle
population	A change project focuses on one aim, in one level of care, with one population, at one location. In this context, population describes the group of clients or the program where the change will be tested, i.e., pregnant women, adolescents, homeless adult males, etc.
process	The structure or series of steps used to perform work
process improvement	Changing the way that work is performed so that it is more efficient and effective
promising practice	Administrative or clinical practice that has proven effective at achieving a specific aim, and holds promise for other organizations.
rapid-cycle testing	One of the NIATx principles, rapid-cycle testing is a way to conduct PDSA Cycles

Term	Definition
referral source	The person or agency who recommends a client to a particular treatment provider
retention	Keeping clients involved in treatment activities and receiving required services. See continuation.
same-day service	Service is available on the same day that the client makes first contact.
site	See agency, provider, site, organization
sustainability	The continuation of an improvement beyond a six-month period after implementation. Sustainability largely involves the concept of continuous improvement, where initial changes adapt and evolve as necessary to maintain the gain. Any change that reverts to the old work process is not considered to be sustained. Examples of sustainability would be embedding the process in policy and procedure manuals, orientation for new staff, etc.
transition	The movement of a client from one level of care to another
unit of service	The measure of treatment service, which varies depending on the level of care. For outpatient, one unit of service is a treatment session on a distinct date.
walk-through	A walk-through is an exercise where staff members walk through the treatment processes just as a 'customer' does.
wraparound services	Services provided in addition to substance abuse treatment, which may include for example, finding and arranging for housing, employment and/or childcare.

168

Index

Recommended Reading

(1999, February). Getting evidence into practice. *Effective Health Care*, 5(1). Retrieved from www.york.ac.uk

Beer M., Eisenstat R.A. and Spector B. (1990). "Why change programs don't produce change." *Harvard Business Review*, 68(6), 158-166.

Berry L.L., Seiders K., and Wilder S.S. (2003). "Innovations in access to care: A patient-centered approach." *Annals of Internal Medicine*, 139(7), 568-574.

Berwick, D. M. (1996). "A primer on leading the improvement of systems." *British Medical Journal*, 312(7031), 619-622.

Berwick, D. M. (1998). "Developing and testing changes in delivery of care." *Annals of Internal Medicine*, 128(8), 651-656.

Capoccia, V.A., Cotter, F., Gustafson, D.H., Cassidy, E., Ford, J.H., Madden, L., Owens, B.O., Farnum, S.O., McCarty, D., & Molfenter, T. (2007) Making "Stone Soup": Improvements in Clinic Access and Retention in Addiction Treatment. *Joint Commission Journal of Quality and Safety*, 33(2): 95-103.

Capoccia, V.A., Gustafson, D.H., O'Brien, J., Chalk, M. (2007) Letter to the Editor. *Journal of Substance Abuse Treatment*, (33): 219-220.

Evans, A., Rieckmann, T., Fitzgerald, M., Gustafson, D. H. (2007). "Teaching the NIAIx Model of Process Improvement as an Evidence-Based Process." *Journal of Teaching in the Addictions*, 6(2)

Ford II, J.H., Wise, M., Wisdom, J.P. (2010). "A peek inside the box: How information flows through substance abuse treatment agencies." *Journal of Technology in Human Services*, 28(3): 121-143

Ford, J.H., Green, C.A., Hoffman, K.A., Wisdom, J.P., Riley, K.J., Bergmann, L. & Molfenter, T. (2007). "Process improvement needs in substance abuse treatment: Admissions walk-through results." *Journal of Substance Abuse Treatment*, 33 (4): 379-389.

Ford, James H.II; Krahn, Dean; Wise, Meg; Oliver, Karen Anderson. "Measuring Sustainability Within the Veterans Administration Mental Health System Redesign Initiative." *Quality Management in Health Care*, 20(4): 263-279, October/December 2011

Garnick, D.W., Lee, M.T., Horgan, C.M., Acevedo, A., and Washington Circle Public Sector Work-group (2009). "Adapting Washington Circle Performance Measures for Public Sector Substance Abuse Treatment Systems." *Journal of Substance Abuse Treatment*, 36(3): 265-77.

Gustafson, D. H., Arroa, N. K., Nelson, E. C., and Boberg, E. W. (2001). "Increasing understanding of patient needs during and after hospitalization." *Journal On Quality Improvement*, 27(2), 81-92.

Gustafson, D.H., Resar, R. Johnson, K., and Daigle, J. G. (2008). "Don't Fumble the Treatment Handoff." *Addiction Professional*, 6(5)

Gustafson, D. H. and Schoofs Hundt, A. (1995). "Findings of innovation research applied to quality management principles for health care." *Health Care Management*, 20(2), 16-33.

Gustafson, D.H., Shaw B., Isham A., Baker, T., Boyle, M. and M. Levy. (2011). "Explicating an Evidence-based, Theoretically Informed, Mobile Technology-Based System to Improve Outcomes for People in Recovery for Alcohol Dependence. *Substance Use and Misuse*, 46 (1)

Gustafson, D.H., Boyle, M., Shaw, B., Isham, A., McTavish, F., Richards, S., Schubert, C., Levy, M., and Johnson, K. (2011). "An E-Health Solution for People with Alcohol Problems." *Alcohol Research and Health*, 33 (4); 320-327.

Hoffman KA, Ford JH, Tillotson CJ, Choi D, and McCarty D. (2011). "Days to treatment and early retention among patients in treatment for alcohol drug disorders." *Addictive Behaviors*, 36 (6): 643-647.

Hoffman, K., Ford, J., Dongseok, C., Gustafson, D., McCarty, D. (2008). "Replication and sustainability of improved access and retention within the Network for the Improvement of Addiction Treatment." *Drug and Alcohol Dependence*, 98(1-2): 63-9.

Kane, R. L., Bartlett, J., & Potthoff, S. (1994). "Integrating an outcomes information system into managed care for substance abuse." *Behavioral Healthcare Tomorrow*, 3(3), 57-61.

Keill, P., and Johnson, T. (1994). "Optimizing performance through process improvement." *Journal of Nursing Care Quality*, 9(1), 1-9.

McCarty D, Gustafson D, Capoccia VA, Cotter F. (2009). "Improving Care for the Treatment of Alcohol and Drug Disorders." *Journal of Behavioral Health Services Research*, 36(1):52-60.

McCarty, D., Gustafson, D., Wisdom, J., Ford, J., Choi, D., Molfenter, T., Capoccia, V., & Cotter F. (2007). "The Network for the Improvement of Addiction Treatment (NIATx): Strategies to Enhance Access and Retention." *Drug and Alcohol Dependence*, 88(2-3): 138-145

McConnell, K., Hoffman, K., Quanbeck, A., McCarty, D. (2009) "Management Practices in Substance Abuse Treatment Programs." *Journal of Substance Abuse Treatment*, 37(1): 79-89.

Molfenter, T., Ford II, J.H., and Bhattacharya, A. (2011). "The Development and use of a Model to Predict Sustainability of Change in Health care Settings." *International Journal of Information Systems and Change Management*, 5(1): 22-35

Morell JA, Hilscher R, Magura S, and Ford J. (2010) "Integrating Evaluation and Agent-Based Modeling: Rationale and an Example for Adopting Evidence-Based Practices." *Journal of Multidisciplinary Evaluation*, 6(14): 18-31.

Ovretveit, J., Bate, P. Cleary, P., Cretin, S., Gustafson, D., McInnes, K., et al. (2002). "Quality collaboratives—lessons from research." *Quality & Safety in Health Care*, 11, 270-275.

Parker, S. S., & Vitelli, T. (1997). "Health care's quality improvement imperative." *World Hospitals and Health Services*, 33(2), 28-34.

Petry, Nancy and Bohn, Micheal (2003). "Fishbowls and candy bars: Using low-cost incentives to increase treatment retention." *NIDA Science & Practice Perspectives*, 2(1).

Plsek, P. (1999). "Innovative thinking for the improvement of medical systems." *Annals of Internal Medicine*, 131(6), 438-44.

Plsek, Paul. (2003). "Complexity and the adaption of innovation in healthcare." Commissioned for Accelerating Quality Improvement in Health Care: Strategies to Speed the Diffusion of Evidence-Based Innovations conference, convened by the National Institute for Health Care Management Foundation and the National Committee for Quality Health Care.

Potthoff, S. J., Kane, R. L., Bartlett, J., & McKee Schwartz, A. (1994). "Developing a managed care clinical information system to assess outcomes of substance abuse treatment." *Clinical Performance and Quality Health Care*, 2, 148-153.

Quanbeck, Andrew R.; Madden, Lynn; Edmondson, Eldon; Ford, James H.; McConnell, K. John; McCarty, Dennis; and Gustafson, David H. "A Business Case for Quality Improvement in Addiction Treatment: Evidence from the NIATx Collaborative." *The Journal of Behavioral Health Services and Research*. September 15, 2011

Quanbeck, AR., Gustafson, DH., Ford II, JH., Pulvermacher, A., French, MT., McConnell, KJ., and McCarty, D. (2011) "Disseminating quality improvement: study protocol for a large cluster randomized trial." *Implementation Science*, 6(44).

Rieckmann, T., Fussell, H., Doyle, K., Ford, J., and Riley, K. (2011). "Adolescent Substance Abuse Treatment: Organizational Change and Quality of Care." *Journal of Addictions & Offender Counseling*; 31(2): 80-93.

Rogers, E. M. (2003). *Diffusion of innovations*. New York: Free Press.

Roosa, Mathew, Scripa, Joseph S., Zastowny, Thomas R., Ford II, James H. (2011). "Using a NIATx based local learning collaborative for performance improvement." *Evaluation and Program Planning*, 34: 390-398

Schaffer R.H. and Thomson H. A. (1992). "Successful change programs begin with results." *Harvard Business Review*, 70(1): 81-89.

Sirio C.A., Segel K.T., Keyser D.J., Harrison E.I., Lloyd J.C., Weber R.J., Muto C.A., Webster D.G., Pisowicz V., Feinstein K.W. (2003). "Pittsburgh regional healthcare initiative: A systems approach for achieving perfect patient care." *Health Affairs*. 22(5), 157-165.

Strom, K.L. (2001). "Quality improvement interventions: What works?" *Journal for Healthcare Quality*, 23(5), 4-14.

The Indigent Care Institute. (2003, June). "Unsuspected eligibilities discovered: Health system nets $38 million by improving enrollment process." *Indigent Care Success*.

Weber, V., and Joshi, M. S. (2000). "Effecting and leading change in health care organizations." *The Joint Commission Journal on Quality Improvement*, 26(7), 388-99.

Wisdom JP, Ford II, JH, Wise M, Mackey D, Green CA. (2011). Substance Abuse Treatment Programs' Data Management Capacity: An Exploratory Study. *Journal of Behavioral Health Services and Research*. 38(2): 249-264.

Wisdom, J., Ford, J., Hayes, R., Edmundson, E., Hoffman, K., & McCarty, D. (2006). "Addiction Treatment Agencies' Use of Data: a Qualitative Assessment." *Journal of Behavioral Health Services and Research*, 33(4): 394-407.

Wisdom, J.P., Hoffman, K., Rechberger, E., Seim, K. & Owens, B. (2009). "Women-Focused Treatment Agencies and Process Improvement: Strategies to Increase Client Engagement." *Women & Therapy*, 32, 69 – 87.

Wisdom, J.P.; Ford II, J.H. and McCarty, D. (2010). "The use of health information technology in publically funded U.S., substance abuse treatment agencies." *Contemporary Drug Problems*, 37: 315-339.